LUKEWARMNESS

LUKEWARMNESS
The Devil in Disguise

Francis Carvajal

SINAG-TALA PUBLISHERS, INC.
Manila

This edition of *Lukewarmness: The Devil in Disguise* is published in the Philippines by Sinag-tala Publishers, Inc., 4/F Regina Building, 100 Aguirre Street, Legaspi Village, Makati, Metro Manila.

This is a translation by Mr. Ted Wills of *La Tibieza*, first published in 1978 by Ediciones Palabra, S.A. and in 1992 by Scepter Press and Sinag-tala Publishers.

© 1992 English translation
  Scepter Press and Sinag-tala Publishers
  Printed in Hongkong 1995

ISBN   971 117 051 5

"I know thy works; thou art neither cold nor hot. I would that thou wert cold or hot. But because thou art lukewarm, and neither cold nor hot, I am about to vomit thee out of my mouth."

Apocalypse 3:15-16

CONTENTS

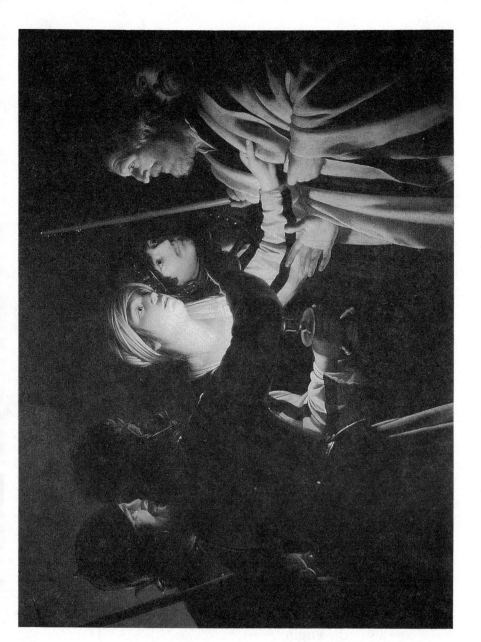

Gerrit van Honthorst, *Denial of St. Peter*, The Minneapolis Institute of Arts.

I

BLESSED ARE YOUR EYES,
FOR THEY SEE

People desire joy and happiness more than anything else in the world. There are many popular expressions of this sentiment in every language and culture. For example, we wish people good luck or good fortune. This is certainly a noble and worthy custom. And yet, all of this wishing does suggest that people are not that successful in finding joy and happiness in their lives. This is true even when people have everything they want, materially speaking.

We may have the impression that certain words like *joy*, *happiness* and *peace* are similar to rare coins. They have an incredible value and are quite difficult to obtain. What we wouldn't give for a month, a day, or even an afternoon of pure joy!

There are those who doubt that true happiness exists. These skeptics have gone so far as to invent substitutes for real joy. They have given these substitutes names which do not belong to them: "tranquility" is called "peace"; "boisterous laughter" is termed "joy"; "fleeting pleasure" has become "happiness." Nevertheless, authentic peace, joy and happiness do exist and they are within the reach of every person. Many people do not find them, however, because they are looking in the wrong places. You cannot find precious stones in a grocery store, no matter how hard you try.

True peace and joy will only be found in God. We will never find them in his absence.

The Lord told his disciples in very clear terms: *"Blessed are your eyes, for they see, and your ears, for they hear."*[1] Jesus called his followers "blessed." He gave them reason to be happy. It was not because of wealth or power or good health. They were "blessed" because they could "see" and "hear" what so many people had long been waiting for. They were "blessed" because they were open to faith in Christ.

In search of joy

According to St. Thomas, joy is the first effect of love and self-giving.[2] There are as many kinds of joy as there are kinds of love. The joy of someone who loves a good meal is quite distinct from the joy of someone who has just fallen in love with another. One might say that the source of one's joy is the home of one's love.

There is no comparison to the joy of loving God. *"The cheerfulness you should have is not the kind we might call physiological—like that of a healthy animal. Rather, it is the supernatural happiness that comes from the abandonment of everything, including yourself, into the loving arms of our Father God."*[3] The Christian is joyful because his life is based on the love of God. It is inconceivable that a committed Christian should live his faith without joy.

---

[1] Matt 13:16.
[2] Cf. St. Thomas, *Summa Theologica*, 2-2, q. 28, a. 4.
[3] Cf. J. Escrivá, *The Way*, 659.

The Christian's joy is rooted in a life of faith, hope and love. This joy can go hand in hand with sorrow, misfortune and material poverty.

Everyone who has had an encounter with God knows the meaning of true joy. This realization can spring from the most varied situations. It will enable us to be faithful. *"Why did you not bring him?" asked the chief of the temple guards. At the risk of their jobs and their freedom the temple guards replied: "No man ever spoke like this man!"*[4] We may recall what Peter said on Mount Tabor: *"Master, it is well that we are here."*[5] There is also the immense joy experienced by the Magi when they found their star once more, their celestial guide to the Child Jesus.[6] The wise old man Simeon was also filled with joy: *"Lord, now lettest thou thy servant depart in peace, according to thy word; for mine eyes have seen thy salvation."*[7] The two disciples on their way to Emmaus were openly depressed until their meeting with the Risen Lord.[8] St Paul reviewed his sufferings on account of the Faith when writing to the Corinthians: *"I am filled with comfort. With all our affliction, I am overjoyed."*[9] The joy of Mary exceeds everyone else's experience: *"My soul magnifies the Lord, and my spirit rejoices in God my Savior."*[10]

We note that there is a special joy in the accounts of the Resurrection left to us by the Evangelists. This was the joy that the Apostles carried with them in the face of hardship and persecution. The Lord's promise at the Last Supper had been fulfilled: *"I will see you again and your hearts will rejoice, and no one will take your joy from you."*[11]

In the days following the Resurrection, every time Jesus appeared to someone we read of the same reaction: *people*

[4]John 7:46.
[5]Mark 9:5.
[6]Cf. Matt 2:10.
[7]Luke 2:29-30.

[8]Cf. Luke 24:13-35.
[9]2 Cor 7:4.
[10]Luke 1:46-47.
[11]John 16:22.

rejoiced at the sight of the Lord.[12] This joy was not based on feelings, good health or any other human consideration. This joy sprang from the wonder of seeing the Lord, of being with him. This same phenomenon was evident at the Annunciation when the Angel told Mary: *"Hail, full of grace, the Lord is with you!"*[13] Her unsurpassable joy is the result of the nearness of God.

We are also full of joy when the Lord is present in our life, when we do not lose him, when we struggle against lukewarmness and selfishness. If we should look for happiness apart from God, we will end up with loneliness and sorrow. This lesson has been proved time and time again. Outside of God there is no lasting happiness. On the other hand, each step closer to Christ is a step nearer to true happiness and the fullness of joy. This is the pearl of great value that is spoken of in the Gospel.[14] To find Christ (and to find him again) brings with it a great joy which is ever new. Nothing can compare with the richness of this encounter. It is worth any sacrifice. Therefore, our union with Christ must be our highest priority.

In Christ is to be found our hope. Our joy and consolation depend on him. "For Christ is alive. He is not someone who has gone, someone who existed for a time and then passed on, leaving us a wonderful example and a great memory."

"No, Christ is alive. Jesus is the Emmanuel: God with us. His resurrection shows us that God does not abandon his own. He promised he would not: *'Can a woman forget her baby that is still unweaned, pity no longer the son she bore in her womb? Even these may forget, yet I will not forget you'* (Is 49:14-15). And he has kept his promise. *'His delight is still to be with the sons of men'* (Prov 8:31)."[15]

---

[12]Cf. John 20:20.   [14]Cf. Matt 13:45-46.
[13]Luke 1:28.   [15]J. Escrivá, *Christ is Passing By*, 102.

Christ's presence among us is the fount of all true joy. *"How can we be pessimistic if Our Lord has promised that he will be with us until the end of the world?"* (cf. Matt 28:20)[16]

Christian joy has a very special nature. It can weather the worst of storms, the darkest of moments. Christian joy can overcome any difficulty. This should be the normal course of affairs for any believer. When we find ourselves unhappy, then something is not right in our soul.

As a rule, Christians should be happy with an interior joy. They are not accustomed to unhappiness, pessimism and sadness. These sentiments are seen as illnesses requiring attention.

Despair and sadness are oftentimes symptoms of an excessive concern for ourselves and worldly things. Egoism always leads to a loss of hope and an increase of sadness and anxiety.

There is no greater mistake than to build one's life upon a poor foundation: for example, material prosperity, worldly prestige, money, etc. *"To all these men and women, wherever they may be, in their more exalted moments or in their crises and defeats, we have to bring the solemn and unequivocal message of St. Peter in the days that followed Pentecost: Jesus is the cornerstone, the redeemer, the hope of our lives. 'For there is no other name under heaven given to men by which we must be saved'* (Acts 4:12)."[17] Whoever denies himself and loses his life for the sake of Christ will attain true freedom. This denial of self enables us to see God because our own ego is no longer in the way. We are reminded of John the Baptist's fervent prayer: He must increase and I must decrease.

The real foundation of joy and the Christian vocation itself lies in putting Christ above all things and the self in second place.

[16]J. Escrivá, *In Love with the Church*, 18.
[17]J. Escrivá, *Christ is Passing By*, 132.

Much like the wildflowers to be found on mountain ranges, joy thrives in high places. Down in the valley of human limitations, this plant will never make it. Sadness comes from the clouding of the grand horizons which God has offered us. We will find true joy when we struggle to lead an authentic interior life.

Faith, the source of joy

Faith is the source of Christian joy. *"These things I have spoken to you, that my joy may be in you, and that your joy may be full."*[18] Our optimism does not depend on human considerations, but on the strength of God.

When we live by faith, we see things differently, almost as God sees them: *"This certainty which the faith gives enables us to look at everything in a new light. And everything, while remaining exactly the same becomes different, because it is an expression of God's love. Our life is turned into a continuous prayer, we find ourselves with good humor and a peace which never ends, and everything we do is an act of thanksgiving running through all our day."*[19] It is through faith that we discover the true meaning of our life in the place where we are. *"He who lives by faith may meet with difficulty and struggle, suffering and even bitterness, but never depression or anguish, because he knows that his life is worthwhile, he knows why he has been born."*[20]

This explains why the Christian should always be happy. He bears within himself the source of real joy. From a strictly human perspective, he may have a good many reasons to be sad, but as a Christian, he will always have

[18]John 15:11.
[19]J. Escrivá, *Christ is Passing By*, 144.
[20]*Ibid.*, 45.

at least one reason to be cheerful: he is a son of God. God, the Creator of the universe, is his father. God has an unsurpassable love for each and every one of his children. So how then can we become sad or depressed? Everything we are and everything we do lies in the hands of our Father God. He only wants our good, both temporal and eternal. He channels all happenings to that end. Yet the fulfillment of his loving desires depends to a large extent on our free consent; whether we choose to unite our will to his Will. Such is the complete abandonment of a child into the hands of a loving father. Nothing could be further from abject resignation.

Once we have arrived at this certainty of the goodness of God's Providence, we will be filled with a deep sense of confidence that can weather any storm, even the most unexpected squalls. Those contradictions which appear repulsive and meaningless to the unbeliever are received by the Christian as a treasured encounter with the Lord. *"How many obstacles vanish when in our hearts we place ourselves next to this God of ours, who never abandons us! Jesus' love for his own, for the sick and for the lame, is renewed, expressed in different ways, 'What is the matter?' he asks, and we reply, 'It's my...' At once there is light or, at least the acceptance of his will, and inner peace."*[21]

Even our very sins should not lead us to despair. They should inspire us to live with a greater sense of humility and dependence on God's grace. *"At the very moment when everything seems to be collapsing before our eyes, we realize that quite the opposite is true, 'because you, Lord, are my strength' (Ps 42:2). If God is dwelling in our soul, everything else, no matter how important it may seem, is accidental and transitory, whereas we, in God, stand permanent and firm. Through the gift of piety, the Holy Spirit helps us to realize with certainty that*

---

[21]J. Escrivá, *Friends of God*, 249.

we are children of God. And, being children of God, how can we be sad? Sadness is the end product of selfishness. If we truly want to live for God, we will never lack cheerfulness, even when we discover our errors and wretchedness."[22] We will find our greatest strength when we put all our trust in God.

In this earthly life, we will never be strangers to difficulty: in our work, in our environment, in our interior life, in the apostolate. Undoubtedly, there will be days when we become worn out, physically or morally. We will experience sickness. We will sometimes have to struggle against ourselves if we are to fulfill our duties to God and others. The greater the threat to our peace and joy, the more we have to rely on this fundamental truth of Christianity: we are children of God. The Lord said to his disciples: *"My sheep hear my voice, and I know them, and they follow me; and I give them eternal life, and they shall never perish, and no one shall snatch them out of my hand. My Father, who has given them to me, is greater than all, and no one is able to snatch them out of the Father's hand.*[23]

Like the men and women of every age, we too will have our share of problems. This is the common lot of rich and poor. Our Lady, the Apostles and the saints all encountered hardship and suffering of one kind or another. So too has every non-believer. *"Beloved, do not be surprised at the fiery ordeal which comes upon you to prove you, as though something strange were happening to you."*[24] Hardship is something to be expected. It is an integral part of ordinary life. Our joy cannot be dependent on some future earthly paradise where there are no difficulties, contradictions or temptations. As a matter of fact, we need hardship if we are to attain a substantive victory. Without contradictions, our

---

[22]*Ibid.*, 92.
[23]John 10:27-29.
[24]1 Pet 4:12.

pursuit of virtue would be hollow. We should remember that birds fly not only due to the action of their wings, but also because of the resistance they find in the atmosphere.

Our joy must have a firm foundation. We cannot base it on transient realities such as current events, personal circumstances, health... As St. Paul wrote to the first Christians at Corinth: *"Let each man take care how he builds upon it. For no other foundation can any one lay than that which is laid, which is Jesus Christ"*.[25] The Lord is the one true foundation that can withstand any challenge. There is no sadness which he cannot remedy: *"Do not fear; only believe..."*[26] Christ is well aware of the pressures and difficulties which each one of his children must endure, some of which are self-inflicted. Christ has a cure for every malady.

If we have faith, our joy is guaranteed.

We need joy

Following his conversion, Paul Claudel would often-times remark: *"Tell them that their only duty is to be joyful!"* Joy is an excellent indicator of the quality of our love for God and neighbor.

Being joyful is one way of giving thanks to God for the countless blessings he bestows upon us each day. *"For God created us to be joyful. We have been made for this purpose. Our joy is the first offering which we make to him. It is the simplest and most sincere way for us to show our gratitude for his many blessings."*[27] Animals do not know how to smile or give thanks. God is pleased when he sees us truly happy.

[25]1 Cor 3:10-11.
[26]Luke 8:50.
[27]P. A. Reggio, *Supernatural Spirit and Good Humor*, Madrid 1966, p. 12.

Our joy does an enormous amount of good for those
around us. People will be brought to God by the testimony
of our lives. Joy is one of the greatest gifts we can offer to
those around us. We need to act like the first Christians.
Their lives of peace and joy, especially in the face of martyrdom, attracted many people to the Faith. *"Families who
lived in union with Christ and who made him known to others.
Small Christian communities which were centers for the spreading of the Gospel and its message. Families no different from other
families of those times, but living with a new spirit, which spread
to all those who were in contact with them. This is what the first
Christians were, and this is what we have to be: sowers of peace
and joy, the peace and joy that Jesus has brought to us."*[28] Many
people will be able to discover God in our cheerfulness.

We ought to struggle to overcome sadness in our life
by paying attention to its cause. This effort can be a
marvellous work of charity for the people whom God has
placed by our side. God wants our home to be cheerful. He
does not want us to have sad and tense homes. When
people say, *"That house is like hell,"* they are saying that it
is a house without love, without joy, without Christ.

A Christian home ought to be bright and cheerful. This
is because Christian life leads us to practice the virtues
associated with joy, such as generosity, cordiality, spirit of
sacrifice. A Christian home makes Christ present in an
extraordinary way among other families and society in
general.

We should bring this serenity and joy to our place of
work, to our friends, relations and acquaintances. The
world is sad and restless. More than anything else, it needs
that joy which the Lord has given us. How many people
have found the road to God through the joy of someone in
love with God!

[28]J. Escrivá, *Christ is Passing By*, 30.

We need joy for our own interior life. It is difficult, perhaps impossible, to progress on the road to God if one is unhappy. St. Thomas says quite clearly: *"He who wishes to advance in his spiritual life necessarily needs to have joy."*[29] Sadness saps our strength. It is the mud which sticks to the traveller's boots. Aside from dirtying the boots, it also slows down his pace. The Book of Proverbs states: *"a downcast spirit dries up the bones."*[30] It leaves one lifeless and without energy. Conversely, *"the joy of the Lord is your strength."*[31] Joy protects us from many temptations and disorders. A soul mired in sadness is easy prey to temptation. How many sins have their origin in sadness!

The joy which comes from God is of tremendous help to our apostolate. We should present Christ's message in a joyful spirit. We can imagine how the Lord himself radiated joy while he was revealing the wonders of the Kingdom of God. Jesus certainly carried within himself an immense interior joy.

This divine joy is *"the state of mind which is absolutely necessary for the perfect fulfillment of our obligations. And the greater they are, the greater must our joy be."*[32] The greater our responsibilities, the greater is our obligation to live this peace and joy so that we might pass it on to others: priests, parents, superiors, teachers...

Lukewarmness: as though blind and 'exhausted'

In the words of St. Peter, Christ is the source of our happiness: *"Without having seen him you love him; though you*

[29]St. Thomas, *Commentary on the Epistle to the Philippians*, 4, 1.
[30]Cf. Prov 17:22.
[31]Neh 8:10.
[32]P.A. Reggio, *Supernatural Spirit and Good Humor*, Madrid 1966, p. 24.

do not now see him you believe in him and rejoice with unut-
terable and exalted joy."[33] Happiness springs from the practice of the theological virtues.

Lukewarmness may be understood as a general break-
down of the theological virtues. Much like sin, it is a special
cause for sadness. Christians fall into lukewarmness because of culpable neglect. They lose their peace and joy. The
image of Christ is beclouded in mind and heart: *"he is
neither seen nor heard."* There is no friendship with Christ.
There is no service for Christ. Everything having to do with
the supernatural is reduced to "doing things" rather than
"loving Someone." The soul is left with an emptiness
towards God. It tries to fill that void with things that
ultimately cannot satisfy. The entire life of piety becomes
tainted with dejection.

Gone is the spontaneity and joy of authentic self-giving.
Faith goes into a state of paralysis because love's ardor has
been cooled. *"Here we have the essence of lukewarmness: lack
of devotion. Devotion might be translated as a commitment of
love, availability and surrender. This lack of surrender or 'bad
will' explains everything. Lukewarmness involves a wholehearted disdain for prayer and sacrifice, a preoccupation with
selfish concerns and comfort, a complete lack of refinement in
dealings with God, a coarse and slothful approach to anything
which pertains to the Lord and a self-centered pursuit of human
respect (cf. The Way, 331). The Christian's path to holiness, on
the other hand, lies in love and devotion, that is to say, in loving
faith and faith-filled love."*[34]

Lukewarmness is a grave sickness of soul which can
strike at any stage of one's interior life. We say that a tepid
soul has "fallen away." It has grown weary of the interior
struggle. It has lost Christ from view. Tepidity always

[33]1 Pet 1:8.
[34]P. Rodriguez, *Faith and Life of Faith*, Pamplona 1974, p. 141.

entails a crisis of faith, hope and love. The afflicted person sees Christ in caricature as an indifferent figure. The soul is loathe to make the same selfless affirmations of earlier times. It increasingly becomes satisfied with less and less devotion.

St. Thomas defines lukewarmness as *"a kind of sadness which makes a person sluggish in the performance of spiritual exercises on account of the effort they require."*[35] Conversation with God is reduced to bargaining, to getting by with as little exertion as possible, to avoiding sacrifice. The soul tries to make holiness compatible with worldly interests. It becomes overcome with exhaustion. Then, the soul yields to a series of concessions. The struggle to improve is abandoned. The soul gives in readily to venial sin. The soul's former friendship with Christ is emptied of meaning. Lukewarmness means *"softness, laziness bent on the easiest, most pleasurable way, any apparent shortcut, even at the expense of infidelity to God."*[36]

It should be stated from the very beginning that *all sicknesses of the interior life have a cure.* The soul can once again discover the "hidden treasure" which is Christ. He gave meaning to life in the past, he can do so once more. The cure comes easier in the early stages of this disease, but it is also possible in worse conditions. We may recall the unfortunate person in St. Luke's Gospel who was *full of leprosy.*[37] There came a day when he decided to ask Christ for a cure and he was healed right away.

Let us also be sure to differentiate lukewarmness from mere physical exhaustion, perhaps brought on by illness, or from a loss of enthusiasm. " *'My enthusiasm is gone,' you wrote me. Yours has to be a work not of enthusiasm, but of Love*

---

[35]St. Thomas, *Summa Theologica*, 1, q. 63, a. 2.
[36]J. Escrivá, *Christ is Passing By*, 5.
[37]Cf. Luke 5:12-16.

conscious of duty—which means self-denial."[38] A person can have a great love for God without feeling any special enthusiasm.

When everything is difficult

Lukewarmness should also be distinguished from spiritual aridity. Spiritual dryness may be the result of past offences or it could be a trial permitted by God for our benefit. The soul can be purified and strengthened by trial. When we experience these periods of dryness it seems as if God has disappeared and that the soul is only "going through the motions." The Blessed Josemaría Escrivá has written in this regard: *"When we feel that we are just play-acting, because we feel cold and uninspired; when we find it difficult to fulfill our duties and attain the spiritual objectives we had set ourselves, then the time has come for us to realize that God is playing with us, and that he wishes us to act out our play with style.*

"I don't mind telling you that the Lord has, on occasion, given me many graces. But as a rule I have to go against the grain. I follow my plan, not because I like it, but because I've a duty to do so, for Love. 'But, Father,' you ask me, can one put on an act for God? Wouldn't that be hypocritical?' Don't worry: for you the moment has arrived to play out a human comedy before a Divine spectator. Persevere, for the Father, the Son, and the Holy Spirit are contemplating your act; do it all for love of God, to please him, although you find it hard."[39]

When the spiritual life is cold and burdensome, the soul may still have devotion. St. Thomas defines devotion as *"a will committed to giving itself to everything that pertains to the*

---

[38] J. Escrivá, *The Way*, 994.
[39] J. Escrivá, *Christ is Passing By*, 152.

service of God. "[40] Devotion evaporates, however, in the face
of tepidity. *"But I have this against you, that you have abandoned the love you had at first."*[41] You have grown soft. You
are not my friend like you were before. The person who
prays despite spiritual dryness may be likened to someone
drawing water from a well, one pail after another (one
aspiration and then another, an act of atonement...). The
task is certainly laborious; but the water is drawn. When
a person has become lukewarm, the imagination runs wild
and prayer is abandoned. The spiritual life bears no fruit.
Lukewarmness is essentially sterile and dangerous. On the
other hand, spiritual dryness leads the soul to purification
and earnest desires for holiness.

Piety is not a question of feelings. If we were to give the
name "piety" to certain emotional states, we would be
abusing the word.

There is no question that sensible feelings and affections
are good and noble in themselves. They are integral
components of the human personality which help us to
relate to God. Nevertheless, they should not occupy the seat
of honor in our piety. They are not the most important
factors. Feelings serve to help us in our piety and nothing
more. The essence of piety is the determined will to serve
God rather than one's mind and heart. Our piety should be
able to endure even the worst aridity, if the Lord should
permit such a situation. It is precisely in these periods that
the soul has the chance to grow in purity and strength.

In our life of prayer, we need to be led by our intelligence guided by faith. We cannot be at the mercy of our
feelings. *"To be led by sentiment is to put the servant in charge
of the house, and to get the master to abdicate. It is not sentiment
that is bad, but the inordinate part assigned to it...*

---

[40]St. Thomas, *Summa Theologica*, 2-2, q. 82, a. 1.
[41]Rev 2:4.

"In some souls, emotions are so much the whole of piety that they are convinced that they have lost all devotion when feeling disappears. Oh dear! I have no piety left; I no longer 'feel' anything!—They only had sentiment: when it is gone, they have, indeed, nothing left. But it is not piety that they have lost; they never had it. If they only knew that this is just the moment to begin to have it!"[42]

With or without the help of our feelings, true piety should come to influence every aspect of our existence in a wonderful unity of life. *"Thus God is injected into all human realities which, without him, would be insipid. The prayerful person strives to do his duty with an unaffected piety. His devotion impels him to work, to happily fulfill daily obligations, even when they involve sacrifice... There is an intimate connection between that interior supernatural reality and the external manifestations of human activity. One's professional work, friendships and social relations, that upright desire to join with others for the common good—these are all the natural fruit and logical consequence of Christ's vivifying action in souls."*[43] False piety is a dead end street for souls. It does not lead to any spiritual improvement at all.

---

[42]J. Tissot, *The Interior Life*, p. 54.

[43]J. Escrivá, quoted by Msgr. A. del Portillo in a speech delivered on June 12, 1976 at the University of Navarra, Spain.

II

SADNESS AND LUKEWARMNESS

> The lukewarm person may be likened to the
> mortally wounded warrior described by an
> Italian poet in these words: *Andava cammi-*
> *nando ed era morto.* He continued walking
> although he was dead.

Carelessness

Lukewarmness has nothing to do with an absence of
emotion or spiritual dryness. Nor should it be understood
as the consequence of a fall, even a serious fall. Even if a
soul should give in to temptation, if it has a true desire for
sanctity, it will get up after a fall. The soul is thereby
fortified by atonement and a greater sense of humility.

Lukewarmness derives from a prolonged carelessness
towards the interior life. The condition of lukewarmness is
always preceded by a series of small infidelities. When
these offences are allowed to accumulate, they gradually
sour the soul's relationship with God.

This carelessness is normally evident in little things, in
a lack of contrition for personal sins, in the absence of a
tangible struggle in one's dealings with God and neighbor.
The life of prayer loses its focus and the soul just muddles

along. The person abandons the battlefield of sanctity for the ease of an imaginary truce.

The state of lukewarmness is similar to an inclined plane that leads the soul further and further away from God. Ever so gradually the soul develops a fear of 'overdoing it' and an anxiety for lost freedoms. The struggle for sanctity becomes downgraded to a struggle to avoid mortal sin. The soul becomes weakened as it increasingly tolerates venial sin. One can justify this half-hearted approach with all kinds of excuses related to naturalness, efficacy, personal health, etc. These excuses help to ease the pangs of conscience in the lukewarm person as he succumbs to his whims, attachments and comforts. What was heretofore extraneous now becomes essential. The strength of the soul is progressively dissipated.

When the soul falls into lukewarmness, its vision of Christ becomes blurred. (He does not appear the same as he did before!) The soul loses its former clarity of purpose and the life of piety becomes an ongoing nuisance, something "that has to be done." Religious devotions are emptied of their true content and become hollow shells. Sooner or later they will be abandoned. They are dead works, a boring waste of time that drive the soul away from its former union with God. The lukewarm person does his norms of piety out of a sense of duty or guilt. As a result, they are lifeless. He may even show a singular zeal in performing these works, but they leave a bitter aftertaste. What was once love of God deteriorates more and more into mere love of the law. What was once love of truth is now merely a defense of the truth. What was once love for neighbor is now, at best, a desire to convert him. Perhaps one still talks about God, but one no longer talks with him.[1]

[1] J.M. Pero-Sanz, *The Church in Time of Crisis*, Barcelona 1975, p. 55.

The lukewarm person has no great devotion to God in the Holy Mass. Communions are typically accompanied by a great coldness due to lack of love and personal preparation. These are not symptoms of spiritual dryness. These are symptoms of spiritual emptiness. Personal prayer is full of distractions and self-seeking. There is no real friendship with the Lord. The task of examination of conscience is either abandoned or done in a routine and fruitless fashion.

More and more, the lukewarm person is weighed down by the difficulty of performing good acts in contrast to the pleasure of doing evil. The soul is saddened by the thought of its lost compensations. It hardly puts up a fight against temptation. The very least of the soul's desires is to grow in love for God (which, in any event, it considers completely impossible). The Blessed Josemaría Escrivá has written in *The Way*: *"It hurts me to see you place yourself in danger of tepidity when you don't go straight toward perfection within your state in life."*[2] The lukewarm soul has no ambition to encounter God.

Lukewarmness leads to discouragement and sadness. The soul is drained of its inner resources. The former desire for the things of God is slowly diminished.

Whenever possible, the soul avoids dealing with God. It tries to spend as little time as possible with him (even during the time of mental prayer). As Pieper points out, *"It becomes a deliberate turning away from, an actual fleeing from God. Man flees from God because God has exalted human nature to a higher, a divine, state of being and has thereby enjoined on man a higher standard of obligation...* (It) is, in the last analysis, a *detestatio boni divini* (Matt 8:1), with the monstrous result that, upon reflection, man expressly wishes that God had not ennobled him, but had 'left him in peace' " (St. Thomas, *Summa Theologica*, 2-2, 35, 53).

[2]Cf. J. Escrivá, *The Way*, 326.

"As a capital sin, sloth is man's joyless, ill-tempered, and narrowmindedly self-seeking rejection of the nobility of the children of God with all the obligations it entails."[3] God no longer attracts the lukewarm person. Little by little, the creature turns his back on the Creator. The lukewarm person is bereft of spiritual energy and stands as easy prey for serious temptations.

He who has shall be given

The words of the Lord find their fulfillment in the interior life: *"For to everyone who has shall be given, and he shall have abundance; but from him who does not have, even that which he seems to have shall be taken away.*[4] St. John Chrysostom has commented on this passage: *"We do the very same thing. When we see that people are not interested in listening to us, and do not give us their attention no matter how much we ask them for it, then we decide to shut our mouths. If we were to continue speaking, we would only make them more inattentive. Yet when we happen to find someone who is willing to listen, we are immediately drawn to him so that we might share all that we have. The Lord put it well when he said: what he seems to have, considering that he does not really have even that."*[5]

The life of the soul demands that we keep ourselves open to new graces. If we struggle to correspond, the Holy Spirit will go to great lengths to assist us. But when our struggle lags, then we become incapable of receiving the graces which the Lord wants to send us. This is a classical principle of the interior life: *"He who does not advance, slides back."*[6]

[3] J. Pieper, *On Hope*, pp. 56-57.
[4] Matt 25:29.
[5] St. John Chrysostom, *Homilies on St. Matthew's Gospel*, 45, 1.
[6] St. Gregory the Great, *Pastoral Care*, 3, 34.

We must endeavor to win God's love every day, since we will continually encounter obstacles which threaten that friendship. *"It is inevitable that we should meet difficulties on our way. If we did not come up against obstacles, we would not be creatures of flesh and blood. We will always have passions which pull us downwards; we will always have to defend ourselves against more or less self-defeating urges.*

"We should not be surprised to find, in our body and soul, the needle of pride, sensuality, envy, laziness and the desire to dominate others. This is a fact of life, proven by our personal experience. It is the point of departure and the normal context for winning in this intimate sport."[7] Each day is a gift from God. It is for us to fill it up with love as we cheerfully enter into the fray.

Our friendship with Christ must be forever growing during our earthly sojourn. The Lord wants to see us fully mature inside and out. He gives us all the necessary graces for our development in the human and supernatural virtues. We must correspond to these gifts by our dedicated effort to improve. Our earthly existence is a time of meriting, of making the best use of the talents we have received. *"We have an obligation to outdo ourselves, for in this competition the only goal is to arrive at the glory of heaven. And if we did not reach heaven, the whole thing would have been useless."*[8] Nothing is more important, not professional achievements, honors, wealth... nothing.

This daily struggle can be concretized in our determination to fulfill our plan of life. We have to resolve never to put aside our frequent encounters with the Lord for the attractions of the moment. We should not be swayed by our changing moods. This battle will also be waged in the way that we live charity. We should try to correct the defects in

[7]J. Escrivá, *Christ is Passing By*, 75.
[8]*Ibid.*, 77.

our character. We should push ourselves to be attentive to
details of friendship, good humor or gentleness towards
others. We should offer up our work and do it well for his
glory. We should do an effective apostolate among our
friends, neighbors and colleagues. We ought to use all the
means at our disposal to insure our spiritual growth...
Normally, this war will be fought out in little things. *"Let's
listen to our Lord: 'He who is faithful in a very little is faithful
also in much; and he who is dishonest in very little is dishonest
also in much'* (Luke 16:10). It is as if he were saying to us:
*'Fight continuously in the appa-rently unimportant things which
are to my mind important; fulfill your duty punctually; smile at
whoever needs cheering up, even though there is sorrow in your
soul; devote the necessary time to prayer, without haggling; go
to the help of anyone who looks for you; practice justice and go
beyond it with the grace of charity.'*

*"These and many others are the inspirations we feel inside
us every day, little silent reminders encouraging us to outdo
ourselves in the supernatural sport of overcoming ourself."*[9] This
battle calls for vigilant love, for a compelling desire to be
united with the Lord throughout the course of the day. This
joyful effort is the exact opposite of lukewarmness and the
sloth and sadness it brings in its tow.

Expecting failures

Our readiness to fight does not guarantee victory in
every engagement. There will be defeats. Many of these
setbacks will be of little importance. Others, however, will
be serious. Our atonement and contrition can serve to bring
us closer to God. Nothing is beyond repair for the person
who trusts in God. Nothing is ever totally lost. We have no

[9]*Ibid.*

right to despair because there is always a possibility of pardon, of a fresh start. Even if we have shattered our life into a thousand pieces, God knows how to put things aright, if we remain humble. As soon as we repent, God will forgive us and assist us. *"In prayer, with God's grace, pride can be transformed into humility. Then, true joy wells up in our heart, even though we feel that the wings of our soul are still clogged with the mud, the clay of our wretchedness which is now beginning to dry out. If we practice mortification the mud will fall off, allowing us to soar very high, because the wind of God's mercy will be blowing in our favor."*[10]

Every once in a while—nowadays more often than not—we read about some madman who has broken into a museum or a church and destroyed a prized work of art. In some cases, he is acting out a mental disorder. In other situations, he may be wreaking havoc for the sake of robbing something of lesser value.

How many times have we behaved in the same way! No one notices. Nobody detects the external tell-tale signs which can prove fatal. But the damage is done. These are the times when we disfigure the image of God in our soul.

A piece of art can easily be damaged to an irreparable extent. But this is not the case with the interior life. Whatever damage that is sustained by the soul can be remedied, no matter how serious.

A lapse or a fall should become for us an impetus to greater intimacy with our Father God. Everything can be worked out with a sincere act of humility. *"Haven't you noticed the way families look after valuable ornaments or decorative pieces, a vase for example; how they take care lest it get broken? Until one day the baby happens to be playing nearby and knocks it over. The precious souvenir is dashed to pieces, and all the family are very upset. But they immediately set about repair-*

[10]J. Escrivá, *Friends of God*, 249.

ing it. *The pieces are gathered up and carefully glued together, and in the end it is restored to its former beauty.*

"However, when the broken object is a simple piece of crockery or just a piece of earthenware, it is usually enough to get some simple rivets, clips of iron or other metal, to bind the fragments together. The pot or vessel thus repaired takes on an original charm of its own.

"We can apply this lesson to our own interior life. When we are faced with weaknesses and sins, with our mistakes—even though, by God's grace, they be of little account—let us turn to God our Father in prayer and say to him, 'Lord, here I am in my wret-chedness and frailty, a broken vessel of clay. Bind me together again, Lord, and then, helped by my sorrow and by your forgiveness, I shall be stronger and more attractive than before!' What a consoling prayer, which we can say every time something fractures this miserable clay of which we are made.

"Let us not be surprised to discover our frailty. Let it not come as a shock to see how easily our good behavior breaks down, for little or no reason. Have confidence in the Lord, whose help is always at hand. 'The Lord is my light and my salvation. Whom shall I fear?' (Ps 26:1) No one. If we approach our heavenly Father in this way, we will have no grounds for fearing anyone or anything."[11]

Enlivened by this attitude, we can make a fresh start with a new joy and a new humility. A person could commit a grave offense against God and other people and still end up very close to God in this life and hereafter. *"Truly, I say to you, the tax collectors and the harlots go into the kingdom of God before you."*[12] *"Experience of sin, then, should not make us doubt our mission... The power of God is made manifest in our weakness and it spurs us on to fight, to battle against our defects, although we know that we will never achieve total victory during*

---

[11]J. Escrivá, *Friends of God*, 95.
[12]Matt 21:31.

our pilgrimage on earth. The Christian life is a continuous beginning again each day. It renews itself over and over."[13]

Humility, sincerity, repentance... and then to begin again. We have to know how to start once more, however many times it may be necessary. God takes our weakness into account.

God always forgives, but it is up to us to repent. Every time we begin again there is such a profound and incomparable joy! We will have to make this pilgrimage many times in our life. This is because faults and frailties are an integral part of our make-up.

Our Lord is not surprised by our failures. Yet he also expects that we will earn many victories as well.

The examination of conscience

Self-knowledge is a must if we are to "begin again" each day in both big and little things. The prodigal son was able to return to the house of his father once "he came to himself," as the Gospel relates.[14] He reflects on his miserable circumstances and on the loving father who awaits his return. Repentance and conversion require an honest recognition of sin. If faults and sins are justified or ignored, then repentance and conversion become impossible.

We can achieve self-knowledge through the practice of the examination of conscience. Through this exercise we compare our conduct with what God expects of us.

Certain authors have likened the soul to an enclosed room. Depending on how wide the window is opened and how much light comes in, we can see how much or how little dirt is present. God provides the light which is a manifestation of his mercy. Without this assistance, the soul

[13]J. Escrivá, *Christ is Passing By*, 114.
[14]Cf. Luke 15:17.

would remain in darkness. It would have no self-knowledge and, therefore, no practical means for recovery.

Because of the examination of conscience and the help of God's grace, we come to know ourselves as we really are (that is to say, as we are in the eyes of God).

The saints have always acknowledged themselves to be sinners. By their correspondence to grace, they opened wide that window which lets in the divine light. God's mercy filled and illuminated their souls.

When the lukewarm person has trouble finding sins to confess, it is not because he or she has suddenly become sinless. The problem is that the window of God's light has been shut and the soul is in darkness. In this sorry state one cannot see the dirt, the misplaced chair, the tilted picture frame nor any other defects, be they large or small. Slowly but surely, the lukewarm person stops examining his conscience or does this norm of piety in a perfunctory manner. He is loathe to confront that which is separating him from God.

If we neglect our examination of conscience because of laziness then our faults and failings will take root in the soul. Little by little, without our being aware of it, we will become hardened to the love of God. Sacred Scripture says: *"I passed by the field of a sluggard, by the vineyard of a man without sense; and lo, it was all overgrown with thorns; the ground was covered with nettles, and its stone wall was broken down."*[15]

In the absence of this examination of conscience and a lively struggle for sanctity, the lukewarm soul becomes gradually overrun with all kinds of harmful weeds that tend to proliferate.

When we do the examination of conscience, we first place ourselves in the presence of God. We ask him for

---

[15]Prov 24:30.

lights so that we might see our faults. Without his grace we will remain blind. Then we evaluate our behavior by the light of God's standards.

Let us be forewarned against *"the devil that ties your tongue."*[16] Pride tries to prevent us from seeing ourselves as we really are. The examination of conscience which is done without humility is an exercise in futility: *"For this people's heart has grown dull, and their ears are heavy of hearing, and their eyes they have closed."*[17] The Lord was referring to the Pharisees who had deliberately made themselves deaf and blind. Deep down in their hearts they were not willing to change, despite the many wondrous signs they had witnessed.

If we make our examination of conscience with humility and in the presence of God, then we will discover the basic causes for our flaws in our charity, in our work, in our joy, in our piety. This recognition will enable us to undertake our struggle with joy. *"Examine yourself: slowly, with courage. Isn't it true that your bad temper and your sadness—both without cause, without apparent cause—are due to your lack of determination in breaking the subtle but real snares laid for you—cunningly and attractively—by your concupiscence?"*[18]

This filial dialogue with our Father God should be followed by sorrow of love, the supernatural fruit of the examination of conscience. We conclude this act of piety with an act of contrition that might purify whatever was improper during the day. *"Always end your examination with an act of love—sorrow of love: for yourself, for all the sins of mankind. And consider the fatherly care of God in removing the obstacles in your way lest you should stumble."*[19] Alongside of

[16]Cf. J. Escrivá, *The Way*, 236.
[17]Matt 13:15.
[18]J. Escrivá, *The Way*, 237.
[19]*Ibid.*, 246.

that contrition we might want to add a resolution for the next day's battle.

The particular examination

Closely related to the general examination of conscience is the "particular examination." *"The general examination is a weapon of defense. The particular, of attack. The first is the shield. The second, the sword."*[20] This is a brief and specific review of a virtue we want to improve in or a defect we want to overcome. This examination helps us to keep our fighting spirit all day long. It is the best antidote for carelessness and tepidity.

It is quite normal that people tend to have one defect which is more prevalent than any other. This defect may stand out because of its effects. It shows itself in day-to-day behavior: in conversation, in decision-making, in ways of thinking and acting. We may choose to focus on our "dominant defect" as the focus of our particular examination. Frequently, this defect is the root cause of many others. If we can conquer on this point we will come much closer to God and, more often than not, closer to our neighbor.

Our spiritual director may suggest to us the focus of our particular examination: an excessive preoccupation with personal concerns, a lack of order which disguises a profound laziness, a lack of presence of God shown by inattention to others, or the absence of small sacrifices which leave the soul at the mercy of the senses...

Two components are indispensable for success in this struggle: grace and spiritual direction. Without the grace of Our Lord, nothing can be achieved in the interior life: *"Ask for light. Insist on it... until the root is laid bare and you can get*

---

[20]*Ibid.*, 238.

at it with your battleaxe: the particular examination. "[21] As to spiritual direction, we need someone who will get to know us well, who will guide our struggle for holiness. The spiritual director receives a special grace from God. He can show us the areas that require our attention which may be hidden from our view. The spiritual director gives us valuable encouragement and spiritual support. His efficacy will be in proportion, of course, to how well we make ourselves known to him. From time to time, he will suggest to us the best way of conducting our spiritual combat and the most effective means of doing the particular examination.

[21]*Ibid.,* 240.

III

TO LOOK AT CHRIST

A well-known Spanish author tells this story: *"I remember one lovely afternoon somewhere along the Cantabrian coast where the sunsets are quite beautiful. People would come there just to watch the sunsets. They would arrive chattering away, but then they would be silenced by the changing colors of the sea. Two fishermen walked up in silence. They stood still before the awesome panorama. Then one said to the other, without turning his head, 'Look.' And everyone who was there heard him. We all took in the spectacle... I am sure that each one of us saw a marvel of his own."*[1] Something similar happens when we are in the presence of Christ. We say to those around us: "Look." When our friends look at Christ, each one sees the wonder that he is searching for. Christ is the only one who can fill the human heart. When Christ is present, everything else fades into the background. As St. Paul wrote to the first Christians at Philippi: *"For his sake I have suffered the loss of all things, and count them as refuse, in order that I may gain Christ."*[2]

---

[1] J. Maragall, *Elogio de la palabra*, Barcelona 1960, II, p. 44.
[2] Phil 3:8.

When Christ is present in the life of the soul, everything takes on a fuller meaning: work, joy, sickness, death. Everything. Jesus brightens our earthly existence and gives us the strength to do what God wants from us. Christian life then becomes a deepening friendship with the Son of God and through him with the Most Blessed Trinity. It finally dawns on us that we did not come into this world just to have a good time or simply to accumulate material wealth. We are here to fulfill the Will of God. We exist so that we might serve God with joy, each one in his own place.

Jesus Christ is the universal point of reference for every man and woman who comes into the world. According to the Second Vatican Council, the Church *"holds that in her most benign Lord and Master can be found the key, the focal point and the goal of man, as well as of all human history."*[3] He who has found Christ and endeavors to follow him is on the right path. He who does not have Christ in view is completely mistaken. To be with Christ, to follow him, all of this entails a specific lifestyle, one that is decidedly cheerful, serene and generous.

Unfortunately, the human heart can be incapacitated with regard to serving the Lord.

When one seeks fulfillment in things of this world

"Let not your heart be troubled. You believe in God, believe also in me" (John 14:1).

Much like in the case of wine, human hearts can improve with the passing of time. They can also go sour, spoil and turn to vinegar.

The human heart is ennobled and enlarged by the practice of generosity, cheerfulness, holy purity, care for

---

[3]Second Vatican Council, *Gaudium et spes*, 10.

details, magnanimity and piety. Conversely, the soul is corrupted by the experience of hatred, quarrels, bitterness, impurity, egoism, lukewarmness... The soul is stunted in its growth and ages prematurely. In marked contrast, we may find that an old person has a young heart. How many delightul examples have we known in this blessed state! Regrettably, we also may have come across a number of people who are physically young but spiritually old before their time.

Lukewarmness has to do with interior degeneration. The lukewarm person is someone who is prematurely old.

The lukewarm person has put real love to one side. His heart is full of petty compensations from his environment. One clear sign of lukewarmness is the tendency to constantly acquire more things, more whims, more needs. All the while, the soul becomes more attached to worldly affairs. Perhaps more than a symptom this is a result: an interior vacuum has been produced which must be filled up by something.

It has been said that the heart cannot be empty. Either it is filled with a great Love or it is vainly given over to petty compensations that will never satisfy. St. Gregory the Great has written: *"The negligent soul suffers from hunger because it wastes its energies on base desires rather than aspiring to the highest goods. Because it does not discipline itself, the soul feels greatly attracted to pleasures."*[4] Thus, the popular refrain comes true: *"he who feeds on crumbs is never satisfied."* The lukewarm person always feels empty. The heart proves as voracious as the stomach. When it is not given authentic love, it fills itself with anything.

God is the only reality that can satisfy the human heart. The heart has been made for an eternal and infinite good. It has been designed to be with God. *"The Church truly*

[4]St. Gregory, *Pastoral Care*, Madrid 1958, pp. 174-175.

*knows that only God, Whom she serves, meets the deepest long-
ings of the human heart, which is never fully satisfied by what
this world has to offer.*"[5]

The lukewarm person evicts God from his heart. He
cuts his former bonds of commitment one by one until he
finds himself alone. Then he wants to flee from himself; he
needs to be busy, to feel useful. We will often find the
lukewarm person engrossed in worldly tasks as if his very
life depended on their outcome. *"This restlessness reveals a
desire to find something glorious as a substitute for the lost
adventure and meaning contained in ordinary activity. The
lukewarm person is no longer inspired by the exemplary and
salvific dimension of Our Lord's hidden life. He now finds that
his daily existence is empty. He is absolutely terrified by the
prospect of that void. This is why he seeks refuge in the 'protection' offered by earthly vanities: those little successes and distractions like the triumph of having one's name appear in the paper...
He puts on an armor to shield him from the Lord's allies in
reading, in sermons, in personal advice. Kind invitations to
return to the fold are deflected away. The lukewarm person ends
up being totally impervious to the message of Christ. The words
of the Lord become annoying and meaningless.*"[6]

The lukewarm person suffers from a rare form of laziness: he is busy with whatever relates to his human interests while being totally remiss with regard to his supernatural welfare. He is not sanctified by his weighty affairs and
accomplishments. Lukewarmness can go hand in hand
with a real industriousness. The contrasting value to
tepidity *"is not industry and diligence, but magnanimity and
that joy which is a fruit of the supernatural love of God."*[7] This
is the joy of wholehearted self-surrender to God.

---

[5]Second Vatican Council, *Gaudium et spes*, 41.
[6]J.M. Pero-Sanz, *The Church in Time of Crisis*, Barcelona 1975, p. 58.
[7]J. Pieper, *On Hope*, p. 54.

Detachment

Jesus was making his way out of a city when a rich young man ran up to meet him. The fellow knelt before the Lord and then asked the fundamental question of human existence: *"What shall I do to inherit eternal life?"*[8]

The fellow was young and uninhibited. He caught up to Jesus just before he left that community. The Lord stopped and the youth knelt down. Everyone was watching. It was a public dialogue.

The Lord began with a general answer: *"If you would enter life, keep the commandments."*

The youth responds: *"All these I have observed; what do I still lack?"*

We have put this same question to God whenever we have been disappointed by the hollow promise of worldly things. Each of us has a hidden thirst which cannot be quenched in this life. Christ has a personal response for everyone.

Looking at the young man very closely (they were face-to-face), *Jesus loved him.*

"You lack one thing." We can only imagine how eager the young man was for the Lord's explanation. Undoubtedly, these were the most important words of his entire life: *"If you would be perfect, go, sell what you possess and give to the poor, and you will have treasure in heaven; and come, follow me."*

The young man was not expecting this reply. God's plans do not always coincide with what we have cooked up in our imagination, in our vanity, in our fantasies. Yet the Lord is right every time. Even though we may be initially upset by God's Will in our life, we can be sure that God has our best interests in mind. His plans are literally

[8]Cf. Matt 19:16-22; Mark 10:27-28; Luke 18:18-27.

beyond our wildest dreams. That rich young man got up on his feet, looked away from the Lord and went off sad. The Evangelist feels compelled to provide some sort of explanation for his behavior: *for he had great possessions*. He was attached to temporal goods. Perhaps he remained sad for the rest of his life.

By means of this encounter with Christ, the interior life of the rich young man was revealed. He supposed that by fulfilling the commandments he had fulfilled the Will of God entirely. When Christ asks him for a deeper commitment, then this fellow realizes how attached he has become to riches. Despite appearances, it turns out that he was not all that attached to the Will of God.

He went off sad. Cheerfulness is possible only in the context of real generosity. As soon as we put ourselves totally at the service of the Lord, then our lives will be filled with peace and serenity. We make this gift of self at certain moments in life when God asks us to keep our hearts free.

"And Jesus looking round to his disciples said, 'With diffi-culty will they who have riches enter the kingdom of God! It is easier for a camel to pass through the eye of a needle, than for a rich man to enter the kingdom of God.' " St. Mark tells us that the disciples "were amazed" at this teaching.[9] The disciples were so stunned that they immediately asked the Lord: *"Then who can be saved?"* Jesus answered them: *"What is impossible with men is possible with God."*[10]

If we do not detach ourselves from the things of this world, we will not reach God. Our treasure is in heaven. The things of this world are only means which rust and moth consume.[11] They are in no way definitive. We can choose either God or goods as our ultimate goal. The heart

---

[9]Mark 10:24.
[10]Luke 18:24-27.
[11]Cf. Matt 6:19-21.

will pursue one of these two courses. The worldly heart has no room for God.

The Christian should make a regular examination of conscience as to whether he is detached from material goods as well as personal desires and plans. He should be vigilant so as not to fall into a life of ease and indulgence which is foreign to the Christian spirit. He should keep a careful eye on expenses and struggle to dominate passing whims and false needs. A Christian should give alms generously. He should be mindful of family and professional responsibilities. *"Poverty consists in large measure in sacrifice. It means knowing how to do without the superfluous. And we find out what is superfluous not so much by theoretical rules as by that interior voice which tells us we are being led by selfishness or undue love of comfort. On the other hand, comfort has a positive side which is not luxury nor pleasure-seeking, but consists in making life agreeable for one's own family and for others so that everyone can serve God better.*

"Poverty lies in being truly detached from earthly things and in cheerfully accepting shortage or discomfort if they arise... We must live thinking of others and using things in such a way that there will be something to offer to others. All these are dimensions of poverty which guarantee an effective detachment."[12]

Thanks to the light of faith, we understand the importance of not becoming attached to worldly things. These goods will not endure the passing of time. The goods of the spirit will last forever. When the heart becomes attached to things, when it seeks its happiness there, then the means have mistakenly become the ends. The soul will end up thoroughly dissatisfied, a prisoner of its erroneous desires.

Our treasure does not lie in material goods. Our treasure is to be found in Christ and him alone.

---

[12]*Conversations with Monsignor Escrivá*, 111.

Purity of heart

A large proportion of the pains and sorrows which afflict the modern world, families and individuals are intimately related to the heart of man. The human heart is capable of both the most sublime and most depraved behavior. *"To the heart belongs joy: 'let my heart rejoice in your saving help'* (Ps 44:2); *repentance: 'my heart is like wax, it is melted within my breast'* (Ps 21:15); *praise of God: 'my heart overflows with a goodly theme'* (Ps 44:2); *the decision to listen to the Lord: 'my heart is ready, Lord'* (Ps 56:8); *loving vigilance: 'I slept, but my heart was awake'* (Song 5:2); *and also doubt and fear: 'let not your hearts be troubled, believe in me'* (John 14:1).

"The heart not only feels, it knows and understands. God's law is received in the heart (cf. Ps 39:9), *and remains written there* (cf. Prov 7:3). Scripture also adds: *'Out of the abundance of the heart the mouth speaks'* (Matt 12:34). Our Lord reproaches the scribes: *'Why do you think evil in your hearts?'* (Matt 9:4) And, summing up all the sins man might commit, he says: *'Out of the heart come evil thoughts, murder, adultery, fornication, theft, false witness, slander and blasphemy.'* (Matt 15:29)"[13]

Interior purity enlarges the heart's capacity for love. God said to the Prophet Ezekiel: *"A new heart I will give you, and a new spirit I will put within you; and I will take out of your flesh the heart of stone and give you a heart of flesh."*[14] A heart of flesh needs to love. St. Augustine has written that *"it is not upright for being harsh, nor does it attain a state of perfection for being insensitive."*[15]

Hardness of heart and interior blindness are caused by impurity, selfishness and egoism. Continuous personal

---

[13]J. Escrivá, *Christ is Passing By*, 164.
[14]Ezek 36:26.
[15]St. Augustine, *The City of God*, 14, 9.

effort and divine grace are required if one is to avoid carelessness and sloth. We need to have a clean heart if we are to draw closer to God and more identified to his Will. Purity of heart is indispensable for realizing the Christian ideal of love and service to others.

The Church has always taught that men and women have all the means to live interior purity in all life's circumstances. Holy purity allows us to see God during our earthly sojourn.

To keep the heart clean we need to practice the virtue of chastity. The Lord has made this a requirement *sine qua non* for progress in the interior life. It has been said that chastity is the gateway of the interior life. It is both the entrance and the exit. *"By divine vocation, some are called to live this purity in marriage. Others, foregoing all human love, are called to correspond solely and passionately to God's love. Far from being slaves to sensuality, both the married and the unmarried are to be masters of their body and heart in order to give themselves unstintingly to others...*

"Holy purity is not the only nor the principal Christian virtue. It is, however, essential if we are to persevere in the daily effort of our sanctification. If it is not lived, there can be no apostolic dedication. Purity is a consequence of the love that prompts us to commit to Christ our soul and body, our faculties and senses. It is not something negative; it is a joyful affirmation."[16] It is a virtue *"which helps us to be stronger, manlier, more fruitful, better able to work for God, and more capable of undertaking great things!"*[17]

We need a good sense of humility if we are to live the virtue of chastity. If we are really serious about this matter, then we must be prepared for a joyful, uphill battle. Pope Paul VI has stated: *"Chastity is not acquired once and*

[16]J. Escrivá, *Christ is Passing By*, 5.
[17]J. Escrivá, *Friends of God*, 176.

for all. It is the product of laborious struggle and daily affirmation." [18]

We have to be vigilant lest impurity corrupt our heart, making it incapable of friendship with God. We have to be on guard against avarice, petty dislikes, petty resentments, delays in forgiving others, egoism in its varied forms... These are the obstacles which demand a habitual readiness for battle. They will not be uprooted at a single stroke.

Our heart should be like good wine: with time it will improve in quality. Whatever is good in a person springs from the heart. Most importantly, the heart is the source of our friendship with God, true charity, understanding and every clean and noble affection.

We should ask the Lord to grant us a clean heart, one that is capable of a refined friendship with him. We want to have a heart that can understand everyone, a heart that can forgive readily, one that can sympathize with people in sorrow. We want to be open to people who come to us for help in time of trial. Let us be a rich source of light and encouragement. Every once in a while, we may want to say that prayer to the Holy Spirit from the sequence in the Mass for Pentecost: *"Heal our wounds, our strength renew; On our dryness pour your dew; Wash the stains of guilt away: Bend the stubborn heart and will; Melt the frozen, warm the chill; Guide the steps that go astray..."*

Together with prayer, let us undertake an effective struggle to keep our heart pure in God's sight. We have to forgive people right away, without harboring any bad feeling. We have to avoid envy, critical spirit and murmuring. Let us love the Sacrament of Confession where the heart is cleansed and becomes capable of good works.

---

[18]Paul VI, Encyclical, *Sacerdotalis coelibatus*, 73.

IV

LOVE AND THE "LITTLE THINGS"

"Routine: the real sepulchre of piety."[1]

Lukewarmness and little things

St. Luke recounts how a Pharisee invited Jesus to a banquet. The dinner was interrupted by an unexpected visitor: *"a woman of the city, who was a sinner, when she learned that he was sitting at table in the Pharisee's house, brought an alabaster flask of ointment, and standing behind him at his feet, weeping, she began to wet his feet with her tears, and wiped them with the hair of her head, and kissed his feet, and anointed them with ointment."*[2]

Simon the Pharisee observes this scene as it unfolds with contempt. He looks down upon the public sinner. Simon comes to the conclusion that this Jesus of Nazareth is not a prophet, despite what everyone was saying. Paradoxically, in the very same moment that Simon is condemning, Jesus is forgiving.

Jesus then said to his host: *"Do you see this woman? I entered your house, you gave me no water for my feet, but she has wet my feet with her tears and wiped them with her hair. You*

---

[1]J. Escrivá, *Friends of God*, 150.
[2]Luke 7:39-47.

gave me no kiss, but from the time I came in she has not ceased to kiss my feet. You did not anoint my head with oil, but she has anointed my feet with ointment. Therefore I tell you, her sins, which are many, are forgiven, for she loved much."

We may imagine that Simon had prepared a great banquet, an expensive repast. Yet what Jesus really valued were the little acts of courtesy which convey a sense of welcome to a guest. Simon did not show good manners to Jesus. He thought it was sufficient to spend a lot on the meal. But Jesus gives importance to good manners and the pleasantries of social life. Affability and courtesy are manifestations of good character.

God wants our love be shown in details. God is not indifferent to our smallest actions. He is delighted, for example, when we greet him on passing a church. He smiles at our efforts to be on time, or pehaps a few minutes early, for Holy Mass. He cares about our posture and the quality of our recollection when we are in his presence. He treasures those genuflections that are done with love before the Tabernacle (This form of adoration can help us and help others to have greater devotion to the Real Presence).

Whenever two people are in love, they show their affection in a multitude of tiny details of attention. The betrothed strives to present his beloved with the best engagement ring possible, as if the value of the gift equalled the measure of his love. The ring is not love itself; it serves as a means of expressing love. Through this simple gift, the man is able to communicate his most intimate feelings.

The interior life is composed of many little acts of love towards the Lord. In the course of our lives, we will have few monumental deeds to present to God. Nevertheless, every day is full of little opportunities to be faithful.[3] This is how we can win over God's love on a daily basis.

[3]Cf. J. Escrivá, *The Way*, 813-830.

We can concretize our spirit of mortification by offering tiny sacrifices at meals, by being punctual at work, by making life pleasant for our co-workers and by taking good care of our tools and equipment.

If we are to become more delicate and heroic in our charity, we will need to examine the little details of our day-to-day social relations. Sometimes all we need to do is listen. At other times we have to put aside personal worries so that we might pay attention to the concerns of those around us. We have to control our temper in the face of contradiction. We cannot be overly sensitive. We ought to be friendly with people and avoid criticizing anyone. We should know when to give thanks. These are things that can be done by anyone. This is the case of each and every one of the virtues. In order to be faithful in little things we will need a lively love for God. This love will be proved in little details.

The lukewarm person neglects these ordinary opportunities. He no longer believes that they can bring him closer to the Lord.

Carelessness and neglect of little things leads inevitably to serious temptations and lukewarmness. Lukewarmness makes us insensitive to the continuous invitations of the Holy Spirit. *"We must convince ourselves that the worst enemy of a rock is not a pickaxe or any other such implement, no matter how sharp it is. No, its worst enemy is the constant flow of water which drop by drop enters the crevices until it ruins the rock's structure. The greatest danger for a Christian is to underestimate the importance of fighting skirmishes. The refusal to fight the little battles can, little by little, leave him soft, weak and indifferent, insensitive to the accents of God's voice."*[4]

Once the soul is on the road to tepidity, life's little details lose all of their transcendental importance. Eventu-

[4]J. Escrivá, *Christ is Passing By*, 77.

ally, even more important things are neglected. Dom Benedict Baur has written: *"This misfortune is all the more fatal and irreparable in proportion as one's downward progress is gradual and hence scarcely noticeable. One grows into the habit of continually greater and more ruinous self-deception and persuades himself that such and such things are not of any importance, that at most they are only venial sins, and so on. It is quite clear that when the spiritual life reaches this state, mortal sin is not far off."*[5] The lukewarm person fails to go to confession on time. He arrives late to Holy Mass on an increasingly regular basis. Because of a lack of self-discipline and mortification, disorder abounds in his work and personal affairs.

Day-to-day fidelity

Normally, all great downfalls have been preceded by an extended history of small infidelities and concessions to evil, of neglect and contempt for little things.

We may recall the sad case of Judas Iscariot. He asked the chief priests, *"What will you give me if I deliver him to you?"*[6] What had happened to the soul of this man? He had been chosen by the Lord himself following a night of prayer.[7] After the Ascension of the Lord, it was deemed necessary to appoint someone to fill the place of Judas. Peter said of Judas on that occasion that *"he was numbered among us, and was allotted his share in this ministry."*[8] Like the rest of the Apostles, Judas had gone out to preach. He probably had seen abundant fruit from his apostolate.

[5]B. Baur, *Frequent Confession*, p. 117.
[6]Matt 26:15.
[7]Cf. Luke 6:6.
[8]Acts 1:17.

Perhaps he had even worked miracles just like the others.[9] And what of all those personal conversations he had had with the Master and the other Apostles! What indeed had become of this man?

Without a doubt, Judas travelled a long road of disaffection from the Master before reaching his final act of betrayal. And it all began with matters of little consequence. There is a suggestion that a full year before the Passion, Judas had grown quite distant from Christ. After that fateful discourse on the "living bread," many of the disciples abandoned the Lord. Then Jesus said: *"Did I not choose you, the twelve, and one of you is a devil?"* St. John immediately goes on to explain: *"He spoke of Judas the son of Simon Iscariot, for he, one of the twelve, was to betray him."*[10]

The split between Judas and the Master must have gradually developed over time as Judas gave way in bigger and bigger matters. He surely resisted the Lord's many invitations to begin again. He must have said "no" to Christ on a number of occasions. St. John provides some revealing information: *"He was a thief, and as he had the money box he used to take what was put into it."*[11] He found within himself a progressive emptiness. His soul had once been filled with love for Christ. Now it was steeped in avarice and longings for all sorts of compensations.

The day came when his friendship with Jesus was finally broken off. Judas maintained an external semblance of discipleship, but the last act had finally arrived. His life of commitment had become a farce. He was only waiting for an opportune moment to sever his allegiance in a violent way. Judas had long forgotten those happy moments he once had spent in the company of the Master and his

[9]Cf. Mark 10:5.
[10]John 6:70-71.
[11]*Ibid.*, 12:6.

friends the Apostles. Everything had become bittersweet. This is the common experience of people who go astray. *"Let no one attribute his collapse to a sudden fall. The explanation lies in following bad counsel, in having abandoned virtue little by little, in giving in to prolonged mental sloth. This is how bad habits gain ground in the soul. Then follows the extreme situation. The same phenomenon may be observed with a house: one fine day it collapses because of poor foundations or due to extended neglect by the inhabitants. Those repeated acts of neglect and omission are like rain drops which wear down the supports of the roof. All that is needed is for a strong tempest to come and finish the work of destruction."*[12] The Lord puts it very clearly: *"He who is faithful in a very little is faithful also in much; and he who is dishonest in a very little is dishonest also in much."*[13]

Our masterpieces of art

It was only a few days before his Passion when the Lord gave us a lasting lesson on the value of little things. As St. Luke relates: *"He looked up and saw the rich putting their gifts into the treasury; and he saw a poor widow put in two copper coins. And he said, 'Truly I tell you, this poor widow has put in more than all of them...'"*[14] St. Mark expressly tells us that Jesus *"called his disciples to him"*[15] so that they might not miss this woman's act of generosity. This was one of Christ's final lessons to the men who would shortly become the pillars of his Church. Jesus wanted his Apostles to learn from a poor and insignificant widow. In the all-seeing eyes

[12]Cassian, *Conferences*, 6, 17.
[13]Luke 16:10.
[14]*Ibid.*, 21:1-3.
[15]Cf. Mark 12:41-44.

of God, she was clearly the biggest donor to the Temple that morning.

For the benefit of his non-Jewish readers, St. Mark pauses to establish the actual value of her donation. Those two copper coins were the smallest coins in circulation at the time. As far as the world was concerned, this gift had no value. The two coins equalled one *quadrans*, that being equal to an *assarion*. The *assarion* was in turn equivalent to one-sixteenth of a "denarius," the basic monetary unit of the period. The average laborer earned one "denarius" for a day's work.

In short, those two coins were practically worthless. Nevertheless, they had the power to attract God's attention. St. Luke and St. Mark were both inspired to record this simple incident out from among the many events that transpired in those final days of momentous drama. They wanted us to learn that lesson too.

The Holy Spirit teaches us in this way that the true value of things lies in our own disposition, rather than in the thing itself. Each and every circumstance and event can be converted into something pleasing to God, no matter how important or trivial it may seem to us. We can attract the attention of Jesus through our approach to little things. We can move the Lord's heart by the love we put into them for his sake.

Each one of us can imagine the many opportunities there are to convert the dullest day into the most heroic episode. We simply have to offer to God the little details of the present moment. Jesus will pay attention to our offering. In this way, everything that happens to us acquires a new meaning.

What difference is there between a well-done genuflection and a sloppy genuflection? As far as God is concerned, the difference is quite significant. The former is an act of adoration, an expression of faith, while the latter is a ridiculous gesture. Similarly, the virtue of charity is oftentimes manifested in little things.

Here is a good example: if we were to stop at a church and make a short visit to the Blessed Sacrament, it would take us a few minutes at most. Yet think of what we will have gained by that brief devotion! Christ repays whatever attention we give to him and does so superabundantly. He bestows the graces we need to continue on our course.

We can make the same point about our punctuality to frequent Confession, about whether we get to Holy Mass on time, about the quality of our preparation for Holy Communion, about the way we observe fasts prescribed by the Church, about whether we remain a few minutes after Mass to give thanks, etc., etc.

Opportunities are always presenting themselves at work and at home. We can accomodate ourselves to a sloppy job or we can struggle to bring to fruition that little masterpiece for the Lord. The lukewarm person is typically careless in whatever relates to God and in many things that relate to men. The saints are the ones who perseveringly offer up life's "trivialities" to God.

The honor due to God

The Christian with a deep faith should show great finesse in whatever relates to God. If we were expecting a visit to our home by an important guest, how would we prepare things? What would our guest think if he were to find our house in shambles: the beds unmade, the dishes unwashed, the furniture out of order, dust everywhere...? Surely he would feel uncomfortable and unwelcome. He would want to leave as soon as possible. He would conclude from the chaotic situation that his hosts had little respect for him, even though a likelier explanation would be that his hosts had grown accustomed to their bad manners and uncouth naturalness.

The sad state of that house may be compared to the condition of the soul which is careless towards God. What would happen if the Lord were to come into the house of our soul and find it a mess? Jesus Christ comes "in person" at Holy Communion "with his Body, his Blood, his Soul, his Divinity." It is the same Christ of Bethany, of Naim, of Nazareth—the son of Mary. *"Simon, I have something to tell you... I entered your house and you did not give me water with which to wash my feet... You have not anointed my head..."* You have treated me quite shabbily.

If we care about honoring God, then we will make sure to receive him in the state of grace. To receive Christ unworthily would be tantamount to sacrilege. It is a grave sin. St. Paul warned the first Christians: *"Whoever, therefore, eats the bread or drinks the cup of the Lord in an unworthy manner will be guilty of profaning the Body and Blood of the Lord. Let a man examine himself, and so eat of the bread and drink of the cup. For any one who eats and drinks without discerning the body eats and drinks judgment to himself."*[16] The Church teaches that *"no one should approach the Holy Eucharist in a state of mortal sin, no matter how contrite he may appear to himself, without first going to confession."*[17]

God's honor calls for us to develop our faith, humility and love. We should want to have recourse to frequent Confession as an excellent preparation for Holy Communion.

These interior preparations should also be manifested in our exterior behavior: by the rigorous observance of the rules of fasting (one hour and not forty minutes...), by our manner of dress, by our interior recollection... Blessed

---

[16]1 Cor 11:27-29.
[17]Dz 880, 693.

Escrivá once had occasion to recall: *"When I was a child, frequent communion was still not a widespread practice. I remember how people used to prepare to go to communion. Everything had to be just right, body and soul: the best clothes, hair well-combed—even physical cleanliness was important— maybe even a few drops of cologne... These were manifestations of love, full of finesse and refinement, on the part of manly souls who knew how to repay Love with love."*[18]

The Lord is waiting for us in the few moments following Holy Mass and Communion. *"If we love Christ, who offers himself for us, we will feel compelled to find a few minutes after Mass for an intimate personal thanksgiving, which will prolong in the silence of our hearts that other thanksgiving which is the Eucharist."*[19] We should not feel rushed in any way for there is nothing more important than being in the Lord's company.

Reverence for God is shown in the details of our actions. *"Piety has its own good manners. Learn them. It's a shame to see those 'pious' people who don't know how to assist at Mass— even those who hear it daily—nor how to bless themselves (they make some weird gestures very hurriedly), nor how to bend their knees before the Tabernacle (their ridiculous genuflections seem a mockery) nor how to bow their head reverently before an image of Our Lady."*[20]

When a person's faith weakens and lukewarmness takes hold, these details are given short shrift. The honor due to God is overshadowed by worldy concerns, laziness and indifference. Carelessness ruins everything. God is not given the respect which is his right.

Jesus was born with nothing and died with nothing, stripped of every garment. Yet when his Body was handed

---

[18]J. Escrivá, *Christ is Passing By*, 91.
[19]J. Escrivá, *Christ is Passing By*, 92.
[20]J. Escrivá, *The Way*, 541.

over to his disciples, they proved their love by treating his body with all the dignity accorded a wealthy Jew.

Jesus had just died on the cross. The disciples had precious little time that Good Friday to prepare and entomb the body. The Sabbath day of rest began at sundown. Joseph of Arimathea went and bought the linen cloth for wrapping the body. Nicodemus came with the necessary spices. St. John saw fit to leave a record of the quantity, perhaps with a measure of surprise: it was "about a hundred pounds' weight."

They did not bury him in a common cemetery, but in a garden, in a brand new tomb. It was probably the one that Joseph had prepared for himself. *"And the women who had come with him from Galilee... saw the tomb and how his body was laid."* Upon their return they prepared spices and balm. The next day was the Sabbath and, in accordance with the Law, they did no further work. Nevertheless, the women were thinking all day long about what remained to be done. The body of Jesus was in the hands of people who loved him. Each one vied with the other in lavishing attention on him. Could anyone have found more loving guardians?

These first disciples give us a wonderful example of generosity towards God. We should not scrimp in anything that has to do with adoration of the Lord.

Jesus is alive in our tabernacles! He is alive, but he is also defenseless, just as he was on the cross. He gives himself to us. We should attend to him as best we can, no matter what the cost in money, time or energy. *" 'Treat him well for me, treat him well!' said a certain elderly bishop with tears in his eyes to the priests he had just ordained.*

"Lord, I wish I had the voice and the authority to cry out in the same way to the ears and the hearts of many, many Christians!"[21]

---

[21] *Ibid.,,* 531.

Just as in human love, our love for God will be shown in our care for little things. Carelessness in these details is a tell-tale sign of laziness, tepidity and a lack of love.

V

JOY AND SACRIFICE

"The lukewarm do not embrace the cross;
they merely drag it along."

St. Teresa of Avila

The lukewarm person loves the easy way

The lukewarm person travels the road that promises the least exertion. He wants the most comfortable and pleasant path in everything he does: in work, in family life, in social relations. His pursuit betrays a profound egoism. One of the first symptoms of lukewarmness is a person's habitual rejection of mortification.

The Lord said: *"Enter by the narrow gate; for the gate is wide and the way is easy, that leads to destruction, and those who enter by it are many. For the gate is narrow and the way is hard, that leads to life, and those who find it are few."*[1]

Here we have two approaches to life: to seek the easy way, what is most convenient and pleasant, to pamper the body and avoid sacrifice or, rather, to fulfill the Will of God at any cost, to guard the senses and have one's body under

[1]Matt 7:13-14.

control. We can live as wayfarers who bring along only what is required or we can live as worldly souls who are anchored to every passing pleasure and comfort.

"If any man would come after me, let him deny himself and take up his cross daily and follow me."[2] The Lord's invitation is as clear as can be. *"For whoever would save his life will lose it, and whoever loses his life for my sake will find it."*[3]

The Lord does not ask for the sacrifice of things as much as he asks for the renunciation of self. This is what has the greatest value for each person: one's own self. The challenge is to live for Christ in whatever situation we find ourselves.[4] The Lord will reward our generosity with the fullness of life for all eternity.

To live for oneself is to court disaster. This life-style impels us towards the *wide gate*, no matter what the cost. All the obstacles to spiritual progress may be traced to this common origin: an inordinate love for self (I come first). This egoism can be manifested in a thousand different ways.

This lifestyle of self-love affects every aspect of our existence. It fosters a distorted interior focus where the main character is always the self. The vain person is usually overly sensitive to what others say or think. He may show a disproportionate concern for his rest and health, for his career, for his future... This self-love may end up being the cause of sickness itself. It always makes a person miserable.

Dr. Josef Pieper has written: *"It is a noteworthy fact—but who has ever called attention to it—that almost all pathological obsessions, witnesses as they are to a disturbed inner order, belong to the sphere of 'intemperantia': sexual aberrations as well as dipsomania, delusion of grandeur, pathological irascibility, and*

---

[2]Matt 16:24.
[3]*Ibid.*, 16:25.
[4]Cf. Gal 2:19.

the passive craving of the rootless for sensations. All these pet-rifactions of selfishness are accompanied by the despair of missing the goal striven for with such violent exertion of will—namely, the gratification of the self. In the nature of things, all selfish self-seeking is a desperate effort. For it is a natural, primal fact, prior to all human decision, that man loves God more than himself, and consequently that he must of necessity miss his very goal—himself—by following the ungodly, the 'anti-godly,' path of self-ishness."[5]

We will find true joy once we forget ourselves for love of Christ. This is the way to peace and freedom. As soon as we stop looking at ourselves, we can gaze at Christ. This was the byword of St. John the Baptist: he must increase and I must decrease. We have to put Christ in first place and our own self in second place. This is the starting point and foundation of Christian life.

Temperance

If a person habitually gives in to his every whim, he will never be master of himself. He will be bored by the things of God and insensitive to many noble human values.

We need to take care not to be swept away by the consumer ethic of our times. Many people have come to believe that material well-being and ostentation represent the highest meaning of life. The ceaseless effort to fulfill these aspirations transforms people into slaves of their desires. *"Temperance leads to self-control, to moderation in the use of material goods. All created things are good in themselves, but they are to be used only for the sake of man's authentic end. Christian temperance is perfectly compatible with good taste and a reasonable level of comfort. This virtue serves to harmonize and*

[5]J. Pieper, *The Four Cardinal Virtues*, p. 204.

educate the sensible appetites. It does not solely restrain them. Temperance thereby orders the appetites to the goal of human happiness as understood in the Christian sense."[6]

Temperance makes man more human. The person who abandons himself to his feelings becomes like a train out of control: the vehicle loses its balance, jumps the tracks and becomes wrecked beyond repair. The higher powers of intelligence and will can be overwhelmed by lower powers such as instinct and the passions. *"The discipline of temperance... is the saving and defending realization of the inner order of man. For temperance not only preserves, it also defends: indeed, it preserves by defending. For since the first sin man has been not only capable of loving himself more than he loves God his Creator but, contrary to his own nature, inclined to do so. The discipline of temperance defends him against all selfish perversion of the inner order, through which alone the moral person exists and lives effectively.*"[7]

The virtue of temperance finds its realization in chastity, sobriety, humility and meekness. These virtues are the fruit of habitual mortification in little things. They are also animated by an interior joy—the very trademark of authentic temperance.

Pope Paul VI has warned us of the danger of the present-day denial of sacrifice and mortification: *"If we know how to discern the orientation of our modern culture, we shall find that it leads to a certain hedonism, to a life of ease, to a determination to eliminate the cross from our pursuits.*"[8] This social phenomenon threatens us all: *"Have we not often felt the temptation to believe that the moment has come to convert Christianity into something easy, to make it comfortable, devoid of sacrifice; to make it conform to the easy and stylish ways of*

---

[6]C. J. Pinto de Olivera, *Temperance,* in GER, vol. 22, p. 175.
[7]J. Pieper, *The Four Cardinal Virtues,* p. 150.
[8]Paul VI, *Address,* 8 April 1966.

the others, and to the way of life of the world? But that is not the way it should be! Christian life cannot dispense with the cross: it is not possible without the hard and great burden of duty... If we attempted to remove this from our life, we would be creating illusions and weakening Christianity: we would be transforming it into a soft and comfortable interpretation of life."[9]

The daily cross

"Whoever does not bear his own cross and come after me, cannot be my disciple."[10]

The wood on which Christ vanquished sin is the pathway to heaven. There is no holiness without the cross.

"To bear the cross" has been a time-honored phrase expressing the sacrifice and surrender of one's life.

The cross is nothing to be sad about. The truth is that the soul becomes filled with bitterness and despair when it systematically rejects sacrifice and pain. The heart becomes forlorn when it is completely immersed in worldly things. Few things are sadder than a life without real meaning. Pain that is not sanctified is a source of sadness. Lukewarmness and sin are sad. Yet the sacrifice that is offered for the sake of Love leads to joy.

When we are next to Christ, our soul can withstand any trial with absolute serenity. *"And he said to all, 'If any man would come after me, let him deny himself and take up his cross daily and follow me.'"*[11]

"The daily cross. No day without a cross; not a single day in which we are not to carry the cross of the Lord, in which we are not to accept his yoke...

[9]*Ibid.*
[10]Luke 14:27.
[11]*Ibid.*, 9:23.

"The way to our personal sanctification should daily lead us to the cross. This way is not a sorrowful one, because Christ himself comes to our aid, and in his company there is no room for sadness. I like to repeat with my soul filled with joy, there is not a single day without a cross—the Cross."[12]

We will encounter the cross of Christ every day of our life. This is not the cross created by our egoism or our envy or our laziness... These burdens do not come from the Lord. These are conflicts produced by the *old man* within each one of us, from our disordered self-love.

Occasionally, we will meet the cross in dramatic circumstances: in a serious and painful illness, in financial crisis, in the death of a loved one, in misunderstandings, in grave injustice. But we will normally find the cross in ordinary life: in the small irritations of our daily work and associations, in unforeseen happenings, in the character of our colleagues, in the little accidents that complicate our plans, in the discomfort caused by untoward weather, in that slight headache which affects our productivity... These are the "pinpricks" of each day.[13]

These small but more or less constant difficulties can be a great boon to our spiritual life. We can use them to grow in the spirit of mortification, patience, charity and true holiness. Conversely, they can move us to rebellion and discouragement. Many Christians lose their cheerfulness by the end of the day, not because they have experienced great contradictions, but because they did not know how to sanctify the "pinpricks" of daily life. When we decide to accept the cross—be it large or small—then we will find peace and joy in the midst of suffering. When a person rejects the cross, the soul becomes out of sorts and despondent.

[12]J. Escrivá, *Christ is Passing By*, 176.
[13]J. Escrivá, *The Way*, 204.

The little cross

We have to approach the 'little cross' of every day with determination. In the morning we should recall that every day has its own cross, a cross which can serve to sanctify us. The Christian who goes about life running away from sacrifice will never find God. Nor will he ever find real happiness. He flees from the forum of his sanctification.

It is by no means easy to be receptive to the cross throughout the entire day. *"For, to despise food and drink and a soft bed is, as we know, a matter of no great difficulty to many, especially to such as are of a rougher nature, or have been so brought up from their youth; and in the case of others natural temperament and habit softens the asperity of such things. But there are not many, or rather hardly one or two, who can put up with contumely, insult, vulgar language, taunts deliberate or indeliberate from inferiors, and complaints heedlessly and unreasonably made by inferiors or superiors."*[14]

This is why we have to ask the Lord for his help. He will give us the strength to take up the cross whenever we abandon it. Usually we drop the cross at the moment we start to complain.

Annoyances will not weigh us down if we bear them for the love of God. Difficulties can dispose the soul to contemplation, to seeing God in the real world. *"So light is the yoke of Christ that, far from being oppressive, it assuages. It is not in the manner of other burdens which, though they have some weight, are said not to weigh heavily—they still weigh something. He who carries a heavy load bends under its weight. This is less true of one who carries a lighter load, although he still feels burdened. He who has no burden walks with an easy gait. It is not this way with the yoke of Christ. It refreshes you when you bear it. And when you put it on the ground, you*

---

[14]St. John Chrysostom, *On the Priesthood*, 3, 13.

feel more weighed down. Take a look at the birds. Observe how they carry the weight of their wings. See how they fold their wings as they glide down to the ground. Their wings might be considered as burdens. Do you imagine them to be so? Yet take away the bird's wings and it will fall to the earth. The less load you leave it, the less it will be able to fly. In a strange sense it might seem merciful to relieve the creature of the weight of its wings. But if you really want to be of help to a bird, don't remove its wings. If you have already taken them away, let them grow back again so that the creature can fly once more."[15]

The practice of interior mortification leads us to discipline our imagination and memory. It is important that we drive away useless thoughts and fantasies. We need to restrain the disorderly movements of self-love, pride, sensuality, etc.

We should also practice exterior mortification of our senses: of sight, hearing, taste and touch. We should avoid pointless chatter and any form of grumbling. We ought to mortify the body: *"The body must be given a little less than it needs. Otherwise it will turn traitor."*[16] Give it less than it needs in comfort, whims, etc. Seek out mortifications that will fit into the context of your everyday life. *"The most accessible realm of mortification lies in our ordinary routine: in our conscientious approach to professional work, in our stubborn perseverance to finish things well, in our habitual punctuality, in the heroic fulfillment of our obligations, in the care we take of our tools and our work environment, in our spirit of service and charity to others. A smile can sometimes be the best proof of our spirit of penance. He has the spirit of penance who knows how to conquer himself in the little things of each day, without making a big fuss about it. This is the selfless love that God expects from us."*[17]

[15]St. Augustine, *Sermon 11*, 6.
[16]J. Escrivá, *The Way*, 196.
[17]J. Escrivá, *Letter*, 24 March 1930, in GER, 16, p. 336.

Through the practice of mortification, we transcend ourselves and come closer to the Lord. Without this spirit of sacrifice, we are destined to remain flat on the ground. Habitual mortification enables us to progress on the road to holiness and friendship with Christ.

VI

WITH THE LIGHT OF FAITH

> "*Amor notitia est*. That is what the ancients used to say. Love makes faith discerning. Love enables the human intellect to enter into God's providential involvement in history and the ordinary affairs of men and women."[1]

Tepidity: acting solely for human reasons

As we have already pointed out, one does not become lukewarm in the blink of an eye. Typically, a person loses his sense of the supernatural through a gradual process. Little by little, he begins to reason and act in a purely human fashion. Faith no longer illuminates ordinary life. When there is no light we become blind and, consequently, we are prone to stumble and fall.

The lukewarm soul follows the most comfortable route. Those exalted goals and commitments of one's youth are firmly set aside. The glory of God is no longer this person's highest priority. What matters now are earthly motives

[1]A. del Portillo, speech delivered on June 12, 1976.

such as caprice, vanity, comfort, reputation, approval... The lukewarm person seeks these consolations at work, at home and everywhere he goes.

In these circumstances, God and his glory get 'second billing,' if even that. The lukewarm soul sees God as an outsider. The Faith plays no meaningful role in day-to-day existence.

For all practical purposes, the lukewarm person does not take God into account. He acts for purely human motives. He will say that his behavior is eminently rational and 'human.' He will point out that this is how other people behave (as if popular customs were the ultimate measure of Christian life). The lukewarm person will rely on his own energy and capability, even though he may have a theoretical appreciation for the importance of divine help and supernatural vision. Yet the theory is wholly divorced from life. And so, God becomes a perfect stranger to ordinary realities. This overly human way of looking at things is nothing less than a loss of faith. St. John calls this the 'lust of the eyes.' We *"appreciate only what we can touch. Such eyes are glued to earthly things and, consequently, they are blind to supernatural realities. We can, then, use this expression of Sacred Scripture to indicate that disordered desire for material things, as well as that deformation which views everything around us— other people, the circumstances of our life and of our age—with just human vision.*

"Then the eyes of our soul grow dull. Reason proclaims itself sufficient to understand everything, without the aid of God."[2] The lukewarm person does not ask for God's assistance. He forgets Christ's words of warning: *sine me nihil*, without me you can do nothing. As a consequence, the lukewarm person has no habit of saying prayers of petition or making acts of thanksgiving.

[2]J. Escrivá, *Christ is Passing By*, 6.

The person who relies solely on his own strength will inevitably be disappointed. Sooner or later, those human resources will fail. The lukewarm person typically has an excessive concern for those personal and material goods that make up the foundation of his existence. His tranquility depends entirely on his natural well-being. If and when his worldly supports begin to totter, then the lukewarm person falls victim to the harrowing anxiety of the pagan. The strictly theoretical awareness of a loving Father God is of little consolation to the lukewarm Christian.

For many such Christians *"what matters in life is temporal reality, the cares of the moment, whatever affects the senses. The supernatural world can be accepted in theory, but in practice it has no meaning...*

"These people live from day to day. Their goal is to have as good a time as possible or at least to avoid much hardship. Lukewarm people work because they have to. If they don't have to work, they won't lift a finger. They see nothing beyond their most immediate needs. They avoid thinking about death. They live for the moment and nothing more. They seem to be waiting for something, though they are devoid of any real hope."[3] The lukewarm Christian is an atheist in the making. The resemblance is truly striking.

A deeper vision of life

Through his relationship with God, man acquires a deeper vision of life. When we see things by the light of faith, we participate in the knowledge of God. Our intellect rises above its natural capacity. We attain to a superior level of understanding. We value things according to their fundamental cause which is God. Only then do we fully

[3]J. Leclerq, *Dialogue between Man and God*, pp. 143-145.

appreciate our human condition: family life, work, health, sickness.

As long as we have the right disposition (piety and a pure heart), we shall see God in all that surrounds us: in the nature of things, in sorrow, in apparent failure, in work... The life of each man and woman is replete with signs of God. If we are to discover God in these realities, we have need of a living faith. This is exactly what the lukewarm person is missing. Without this faith, even the most extraordinary signs would be emptied of value. These signs from God would perish in a complete vacuum.

The lukewarm person becomes blind to the supernatural. In contrast, the person with a lively interior life knows how to find God in the most trying of times. We may recall that some of the Jews were not converted even after they had witnessed the resurrection of Lazarus.[4] Instead of being won over to the Lord, those people reacted to the miracle by moving farther away from Christ. Paradoxically, it is when the Lord's divinity is most concealed on Calvary that a common thief responds to divine grace.[5]

When we have supernatural vision we are able to see God in our life. We learn how to treasure what is most important. Death is revealed to be a step, a transition to God our Father. It is a new beginning rather than a tragic ending. The faithful Christian learns to prize faith above everything else. This is true realism. *"The Christian is a realist. His supernatural and human realism helps him appreciate all the aspects of his life: sorrow and joy, his own and other people's suffering, certainty and doubt, generosity and selfishness. The Christian experiences all this, and he confronts it all, with human integrity and with the strength he receives from God."*[6]

---

[4]Cf. John 11:46.
[5]Cf. Luke 23:42.
[6]J. Escrivá, *Christ is Passing By*, 60.

Supernatural vision helps us to recognize that other people are sons and daughters of God. We will therefore treat them with the respect that they deserve. This outlook leads us to realize that our professional work is the forum of our sanctification. *"There is no such thing as failure if you act with a right intention, wanting to fulfill God's will and counting always on his grace and your own nothingness."*[7] If we are truly united to God, there is absolutely nothing in the world that can separate us from him.

Christians should have this kind of supernatural vision impregnate their whole existence. Then personal conduct will no longer be driven by impulse, by the desire of being popular, by the pursuit of wealth... Instead, we will be dedicated to fulfilling the Will of God. This is how our love of God becomes reality. This is how we prove our loyalty to God through thick and thin. Our code of conduct is to do whatever God wants.

God reveals his Will through the Commandments of the Law, through the regulations and commandments of Holy Mother Church and through the duties proper to our vocation and state in life.

The duties of one's state in life are a very clear expression of God's Will for each person. Our sanctity is intimately bound up with our fulfillment of these obligations with absolute fidelity.

To acknowledge and love the divine Will in these duties is to know the purpose of our life at each moment. Thus we can transcend any mere human ambitions while simultaneously performing our obligations to perfection. It is through these duties that we can grow in both the supernatural and human virtues. As a result, everything around us contributes in some way to the work of our sanctification.

[7] *Ibid.*, 76.

God reveals his Will in whatever happens to us. We need to keep in mind that God always has our best interests in mind: *"We know that in everything God works for good with those who love him."*[8] Everything has been arranged so as to contribute to our salvation. This teaching applies to events that transpire on a grand scale and those which affect our personal world. Everything can and should draw us to God's peace.

We should learn how to see God's loving Providence in those developments which go against our thoughts and desires. It is our common experience that life does not always proceed according to our carefully laid-out plans. If we live without faith, we will have little hope of lasting serenity.

We need to look with eyes of faith at all the events, things and persons in our environment. We will thereby avoid any slide into dejection or sadness. *"The wholehearted acceptance of the will of God is the sure way of finding joy and peace: happiness in the cross. It's then we realize that Christ's yoke is sweet and that his burden is not heavy."*[9]

God is to found in the immense wave of favors and graces that we receive each day. Thanks to supernatural vision, we will realize that our reasons for joy always exceed our reasons for worry. We will be moved to a continuous prayer of thanksgiving. Much like the person whose faith is dead, the lukewarm person does not appreciate the many motives he has for thanking God.

Giving thanks

If we look with the eyes of faith, we shall find that our life is a marvellous testimony to the infinite mercy of God.

[8]Rom 8:28.
[9]J. Escrivá, *The Way*, 758.

We will only find reasons for giving thanks, even in our darkest hours.

The Lord is waiting expectantly for our gratitude. This is a recurring theme in the Gospels.

In the midst of his final journey to Jerusalem, Christ had occasion to pass between Samaria and Galilee. St. Luke records that when Jesus entered a certain village he was met by ten lepers who *stood at a distance.*[10]

Among these lepers there was a Samaritan. Despite the age-old enmity between the Jews and the Samaritans, misery has brought these traditional adversaries together.

Together they *"lifted up their voices"*—they were standing a little ways off—and they offered their humble prayer to the Lord: *"Jesus, Master, have mercy on us."*

Christ and his party were only a short distance from the lepers. Christ tells the ten supplicants to go and show themselves to the priests. This was in accordance with the precepts of the Law whenever a leper was cured.[11] The ten lepers obeyed Christ's instructions and all were cured.

These men must have been overwhelmed with joy at their newfound health. In the midst of their celebration and euphoria, only one of the group—the Samaritan—*"turned back, praising God with a loud voice."* This homage must have taken Christ's disciples by surprise. The Samaritan's second meeting with the Lord is described with these words: *"he fell on his face at Jesus' feet, giving him thanks."*

This is a most beautiful act. *"What better words might we have on our hearts, pronounce with our lips, write with a pen than the words 'thanks be to God.' Nothing can be said with greater brevity, nor heard with greater gladness, nor felt with greater uplift, nor done to greater benefit."*[12]

---

[10]Cf. Luke 17:11-19.
[11]Cf. Lev 14:2.
[12]St. Augustine, *In Epist.,* 72.

Jesus must have been delighted by the explicit gratitude of this man. At the same time, he wondered about the absence of the other nine men: *"Was no one found to return and give praise except this foreigner?"*

Jesus was expecting all ten of the group. Yet they had only remembered him in this hour of affliction. Perhaps later on they convinced themselves that their cure was something natural, or that it was something they deserved by right. Such is the behavior of the lukewarm person in the face of the immensity of God's mercy.

And what about us? Might we count ourselves among the nine ungrateful ones? It is so easy to think of life as anything but a gift from God. The fact that we have been born, the fact that we can see, that our loved ones have life and good health, the fact that we have food on the table... Do we realize that God has bent over backwards for us, providing gifts that we do not deserve: the gift of life, the Redemption, the Holy Eucharist, the constant attention of the Holy Spirit...? Everything we have is a free gift from God. Absolutely everything.

If we take a close look at our behavior, it is not hard to recognize ourselves as the "servant who did not have with which to pay." There is only one thing which we can do: give thanks continuously. As St. Paul wrote to the first Christians of Thessalonia: *"Give thanks in all circumstances; for this is the will of God in Christ Jesus for you."*[13]

We human beings receive many gifts from God. St. John Chrysostom has written: *"He showers us with many gifts, most of which we are not aware of."*[14] Our whole life is a pure gift of God. One day—on that final day—we shall understand that our life has been filled with innumerable gifts from God, so many that they *"exceed the grains of sand on a sea-*

[13]1 Thess 5:18.
[14]St. John Chrysostom, *Homilies on St. Matthew's Gospel*, 25, 4.

shore. "[15] Acknowledging these divine gifts requires a great faith. The lukewarm person does not take note of these gifts. They seem 'natural' to him, since he dwells on a very superficial level. The lukewarm person imagines that he is self-sufficient. He forgets that to be alive is a gift of God. *"There is no one who, on a little reflection, will not easily find in himself many powerful reasons for being grateful to God...*

"Once we have a sense of all that God has given us, then we shall be inspired to give thanks as much as possible."[16]

Everything that happens to us can be reason for thanksgiving. *"Make it a habit to raise your heart to God, in acts of thanksgiving, many times a day. Because he gives you this and that... Because someone has despised you... Because you don't have what you need, or because you do have it.*

"And because he made his Mother, who is also your Mother, so beautiful. Because he created the sun and the moon and this animal or that plant. Because he made that man eloquent and you he left slow of speech...

"Thank him for everything, because everything is good."[17]

How human and how divine it is to be grateful! And it takes so little to show it! It is enough to pause a few moments so that we might back off from our pride and laziness. There we will find Christ waiting for us.

The Samaritan who returned to give thanks left with an even greater reward: the gift of faith and friendship with Christ. Jesus said to him: *"Rise and go your way; your faith has made you well."*

The nine ungrateful fellows missed out on the best part of what the Lord had in store for them. *"For to him who humbly acknowledges his debt and is grateful for his blessings, much will be given. He who is faithful in little will be entrusted*

---

[15]*Ibid.*
[16]St. Bernard, *Homily on the Sixth Sunday after Pentecost,* 25, 4.
[17]J. Escrivá, *The Way,* 268.

with more responsibilities, as is fitting and proper. In contrast,
he who is ungrateful for what he has been given becomes
unworthy of additional favor."[18]

Each time we give thanks to God we end up winning
greater gifts from him.

In the presence of the Lord

Supernatural vision enables us to see God as a friendly
spectator upon our life's progress. He is always ready to
lend a hand to help us along. We come to feel like a
character in a play that is put on before his divine presence.
We play the part which he has assigned to us.

The actor on stage knows that he is in the presence of
an audience. The footlights may prevent him from seeing
the people, but he can feel their presence a few feet away
in the darkness of the theater. He knows that they are
present, that they are interested in the play and in his performance. The people want to see a good production. This
impels the actor to push himself to the limit, to perform
with skill and enthusiasm. He studies each and every move,
every gesture, every phrase because 'he owes it to his
public.'

The day might come where the actor is in the middle
of the show and he senses that the audience is not paying
attention or that the people have walked out. This might
cause him to act in any old manner, without his former
dedication. The actor might even leave the stage in mid-
scene. This is exactly what happens when people become
lukewarm. The lukewarm person forgets that Christ is
following his life with great interest.[19]

---

[18]St. Bernard, *Homily on Psalm 50*, 4, 1.
[19]Luke 10:41-42.

The lukewarm person abandons the production. He no longer lives in the presence of God. Our life would be completely transformed if we lived according to that reality. This attitude would help us to do away with any sense of routine. It would not matter what role we received from God since our one goal would be to please the Lord.

If we are to have presence of God in our life, we need to be prayerful souls. We need to guard our senses, ever-mindful of the great treasure we carry within us. "*Do you not know that you are God's temple and that God's Spirit dwells in you?*"[20]

Our presence of God depends on whether we control our imagination. St. Teresa used to refer to the imagination as the "mad woman of the house." We must control our imagination, otherwise interior progress will prove impossible. The imagination "*is as wild as a horse without a bridle; as giddy as a butterfly; if you fail to control and guide her, you will never be a supernatural and interior soul. If you do not control her, you will never enjoy the serene calm which is so necessary for loving God. If you don't put a brake on her, you will never have that realism which a life of holiness requires. Calm, realism, serenity, objectivity: these are virtues born where the tyranny of the imagination is buried; virtues which grow and bear fruit in the ascetical effort of dominating and controlling your imagination.*"[21]

If we are to guard our imagination, we have to guard our senses. A person who leaves his senses awake will put his soul to sleep. "*Dissipation. You slake your senses and faculties at whatever puddle you meet on the way. And then you experience the results: unsettled purpose, scattered attention, deadened will, aroused concupiscence.*

[20]1 Cor 3:16.
[21]S. Canals, *Jesus as Friend*, pp. 70-71.

"Subject yourself again seriously to a plan that will make you lead a christian life. Otherwise you'll never do anything worthwhile."[22]

"A little diversion! You've got to have a change! So you open your eyes wide to let in images of things, or you squint because you're nearsighted!

"Close them altogether! Have interior life, and you'll see the wonders of a better world, a new world with undreamed-of color and perspective... and you'll draw close to God. You'll feel your weaknesses; and you'll become more God-like... with a godliness that will make you more of a brother to your fellow men by bringing you closer to your Father."[23]

This recollection is perfectly compatible with our work, our family life, our social relations... By their very nature, human affairs have a profound dimension which is ordered to God—unless we let them become cheapened by frivolity. Recollection, therefore, should be seen in a thoroughly positive light. We have to control our senses and faculties. We have to direct our energies to our highest end: the presence of God. Without this realization, we will never have a supernatural vision of our life.

[22]J. Escrivá, *The Way*, 375.
[23]J. Escrivá, *The Way*, 283.

VII

THE DAUGHTERS
OF LUKEWARMNESS

Lukewarmness has six daughters, according to St. Gregory the Great and St. Thomas Aquinas.[1] These sins and forms of disaffection may be listed as:

1) *Lack of hope.* In other words, discouragement and lack of interest in the things of God. The lukewarm person seems unable to lead a mature and demanding interior life. He finds himself "without energy."

2) *An uncontrolled imagination.* The lukewarm person gives free rein to the imagination. He takes refuge there amidst his false exploits and triumphs. He basks in a false happiness that is far removed from the real joy to be experienced by living ordinary life in the presence of God.

3) *Mental torpor and sloth.* The soul is lazy at the prospect of the supernatural struggle. *"When it is not jolted by timely ardor, the soul becomes overcome with*

---

[1]St. Thomas, *Summa Theologica*, 2-2, q. 35, 4 ad 2; *De Malo*, q. 11, a. 4.

lethargy, thereby bringing about the total collapse of any desire for the good..."[2]

4) *Pusillanimity*. The spirit of the lukewarm person shrinks in the face of any supernatural enterprise. The affected soul gives way to many sins of omission and disregards graces bestowed by the Holy Spirit.

5) *Rancor and critical spirit*. The lukewarm person becomes annoyed by people who are struggling for sanctity. He does not want to change his own conduct. The lukewarm person convinces himself that all the problems of the world lie in other people. Good people may encourage him to return to the right path, but the lukewarm person dismisses this assistance as coming from unsuitable teachers— *tamquam importunos monitores*.[3] This attitude can lead the lukewarm person to a hatred of spiritual goods in and of themselves.

6) *An ill-tempered antagonism*. This problem can readily fester and develop into a positive evil. It is nothing more than an absolute hatred of everything that is divine in man. The lukewarm person makes a conscious, internal decision to do evil for its own sake. This is one of the most serious sins which a human being can commit.

Discouragement

The lukewarm person becomes dejected because he has lost sight of the light of his life, thanks to his own negligence. God was once the beginning and the end of his

---

[2]St. Gregory the Great, *Pastoral Care*.
[3]Cf. D. Prummer, *Handbook on Moral Theology*, 435.

actions. Now the Creator has been replaced by created things. As a result, these things come to acquire an absolute importance. *"If we transform our temporal projects into ends in themselves and blot out from our horizon our eternal dwelling place and the end for which we have been created, which is to love and praise the Lord and then to possess him forever in Heaven, then our most brilliant endeavors turn traitor, and can even become a means of degrading our fellow creatures. Remember that sincere and well-known exclamation of St. Augustine, who had such bitter experience when God was unknown to him and he was seeking happiness outside God: 'You have made us for yourself, O Lord, and our hearts are restless till they rest in you!' (Confessions, 1, 1). Perhaps there is no greater tragedy for man than the sense of disillusionment he suffers when he has corrupted or falsified his hope, by placing it in something other than the one Love which satisfies without ever satiating."*[4]

"Let us pray and work with good will, with upright motives and with our sights set on what God wants."[5] Then we will understand that all earthly goods have a relative value. They have to be subordinated to the higher good of eternal life and whatever contributes to that end. The Christian's hope transcends everything that is earthly in an absolute way.

This hope-filled attitude towards life presupposes a constant, cheerful struggle since it is the tendency of every man is to be attached to 'that which is below.' Men and women are forever trying to build the 'permanent city.' *"If we don't fight against ourselves; if we don't rebuff once and for all the enemies lodged within our interior fortress—pride, envy, the concupiscence of the flesh and of the eyes, self-sufficiency, and the wild craving for licentiousness; if we abandon this inner struggle, our noblest ideals will wither 'like the bloom on the*

[4]J. Escrivá, *Friends of God*, 208.
[5]*Ibid.*, 217.

*grass; and when the scorching sun comes up the grass withers,
and the bloom falls, and all its fair show dies away' (Jas 1:10-
11). Then, all you need is a tiny crevice and discouragement and
gloom will creep in, like encroaching poisonous weeds."*[6]

Letting oneself be helped

St. Luke recorded a memorable story concerning discouragement and its remedy in his account of the two
disciples on the road to Emmaus. They had lost all hope
because Christ had died. Jesus joins them as one more
traveller whom they did not recognize. The conversation
has a halting character to it because they were travelling
along by foot. The two disciples share their gloom with
their newfound companion: what had happened in Jerusalem those past few days, especially the execution of Christ.

The two disciples are overcome by sadness, despair and
uncertainty. It is apparent from their conversation that this
Jesus had meant everything to them. Now they had lost
him, or so it seemed. He had died and life had lost all
meaning. They said, "But we had hoped that he was the one
to redeem Israel." Now there was nothing to live for. They
speak of Jesus as if he were a thing of the past: *"Concerning
Jesus of Nazareth, who was a prophet mighty in deed and word
before God and all the people..."*[7]

*"What a striking contrast! They spoke of Jesus in the past
tense... 'who was'! And he was walking right alongside of them!
He is present in their company, asking about the reasons for their
sadness!.*

*"Jesus 'was' for them. If we were to make a serious exami-
nation of conscience about our own sadness, discouragement and*

[6]*Ibid.*, 211.
[7]Luke 24:21

setbacks, we would hear an echo of that same reaction in our-
selves. 'Who was...' 'Who said...' 'Who commanded...' Much like
those two disciples, we too can forget that Jesus is by our side.
He is alive. Once we rediscover Jesus in this way, we will have
a renewed faith and hope. This recognition will be a source of great
joy: Jesus is. Jesus wants. Jesus says. Jesus commands. Today,
right now."[8]

These two men knew that Christ had promised to rise
again on the third day. They had even seen the holy women
upon their return from the empty tomb. Surely they had
been given sufficient reason to hope in Christ's Resurrection. Nevertheless, they spoke of Christ as someone dead
and gone. These two disciples are perfect examples of
discouragement due to lack of faith. They rested too much
hope on their limited human understanding. Consequently, their minds were shackled and their hearts were
closed to the supreme reality of God's omnipotence.

Amazingly enough, it is Christ himself who walks with
them as they walk away from the Resurrection. With infinite patience and love, Christ teaches his disciples once
again the meaning of the Scriptures and the sufferings of
the Messiah. The Risen Christ brings his two disciples back
to life. After Jesus vanishes from their sight, they exclaim,
"Did not our hearts burn within us while he talked to us on the
road, while he opened to us the Scriptures?"[9]

We are no strangers to discouragement in this life. But
Jesus will not let us walk away discouraged. Someone will
come along with us to explain the Scriptures. We will have
clarity of vision again. Our heart will burn with renewed
faith in Christ. Perhaps only then will we realize that Christ
was always by our side, even when we imagined that he
was far, far away. We will see the Lord more clearly if we

[8]A.G. Dorronsoro, *God and People*, Madrid 1973, p. 103.
[9]Luke 24:32

regularly receive spiritual direction. As soon as we do see him, we will be filled with joy and a great desire to begin again without delay. So it was with the two disciples who had been heading for Emmaus. *"And they rose that same hour and returned to Jerusalem..."*

In our apostolate, we will probably meet people who have lost their supernatural bearings in life. We have to lead them—in Christ's Name—to light and to hope. For there is so much lukewarmness in the world, so much darkness!

The Lord is always offering us his friendship. No matter how many times we have offended him, no matter how lukewarm we have been, the Lord is eager to forgive us. *"If the forgiveness we need had to be won by our own merits, we would only be capable of a bitter sadness. But, because of God's goodness, forgiveness comes from his mercy..."*[10] This is the firm foundation of our hope: Jesus desires our friendship. He well knows the depth of man's frailty. He showers us with his grace so that we might correspond and begin again. *"Sometimes, when things turn out the very opposite of what we intended, we cry out spontaneously: 'Lord, it's all going wrong, every single thing I'm doing!' The time has come for us to rectify our approach and say: 'With you, Lord, I will make steady headway, because you are strength itself, quia tu es Deus fortitudo mea' (Ps 42:2)."*[11]

It is of the utmost importance that we keep our sights fixed on Heaven. *"Hope encourages us to grasp hold of the strong hand which God never ceases to reach out to us, to keep us from losing our supernatural point of view,"* wrote the Blessed Josemaría Escrivá: *"Let us persevere even when our passions rear up and attack us, attempting to imprison us within the narrow confines of our selfishness; or when puerile vanity*

---

[10]J. Escrivá, *Christ is Passing By*, 88.
[11]*Idem., Friends of God*, 213.

makes us think we are the center of the universe. I am convinced that unless I look upward, unless I have Jesus, I will never accomplish anything. And I know that the strength to conquer myself and to win comes from repeating that cry, 'I can do all things in him who strengthens me' (Phil 4:13), words which reflect God's firm promise not to abandon his children if they do not abandon him."[12]

Pusillanimity

The *Book of Numbers* relates how Yahweh instructed Moses to send out men to reconnoiter the Promised Land, which had still to be conquered by the Chosen People.[13]

Twelve scouts went forth who represented the different tribes of Israel. They spent forty days studying the fertility of the land and the military resources of its inhabitants. The scouts reported back to Moses that the land "flowed with milk and honey." At the same time, they expressed their fears about the enemy forces: *"The people who dwell in the land are strong, and the cities are fortified and very large."* Here they committed a grave miscalculation. For in their comparisons of military strength, they had neglected to take into account the tremendous power of God. After all, it was God who had reserved this land for his Chosen People. Had not Yahweh always been generous to Israel in the past?

How quickly these young men were to forget the divine character of their enterprise. These scouts had succumbed to a merely human vision of the conquest of Canaan. They even brought home an exaggerated account of the enemy's strength which further dismayed the Chosen People. The scouts reported: *"The land, through which we have gone to spy*

[12]*Ibid.*, 213.
[13]Num 13 and 14 ff.

it out, is a land that devours its inhabitants; and all the people that we saw in it are men of great stature... We seemed to ourselves like grasshoppers, and so we seemed to them." This frightful news broke the spirit of the people of Israel. *"And they said to one another, 'Let us choose a captain, and go back to Egypt'."* The Chosen People went into open rebellion against the Lord and his servant Moses.

Yahweh had never failed to assist his people before. He appeared to Moses in the tent of meeting and said, *"How long will this people despise me?"* Truly, to exhibit such a lack of faith is a serious offence against God. If we do not rest our hopes in the Lord, we will not accomplish any supernatural undertaking.

As punishment for their lack of faith, Yahweh decreed that the Chosen People were to wander in the desert for another forty years. There was, however, one exception. The Lord said to Moses, *"But my servant Caleb, because he has a different spirit and has followed me fully, I will bring into the land into which he went, and his descendants shall possess it. Now, since the Amalekites and the Canaanites dwell in the valleys, turn tomorrow and set out for the wilderness by the way to the Red Sea."*

The Lord explained his punishment with these words: *"According to the number of the days in which you spied out the land, forty days, for every day a year, you shall bear your iniquity, forty years, and you shall know my displeasure."*

In much the same manner, the lukewarm soul is aware of what God has prepared for it as well as what God expects from it. Yet the lukewarm person does not go forward into the Promised Land. It wanders about in the desert of mediocrity and self-love. The lukewarm soul has no set destination. It bears no fruit. The lukewarm person becomes more and more cowardly, having neither the courage nor the desire to follow God's Will. This soul prefers to lower its sights from divine goals to human goals.

"*Fundamentally, what is wrong with it is that there is no real desire to achieve anything worthwhile, either spiritual or material. Thus some people's greatest ambition boils down to avoiding whatever might upset the apparent calm of their mediocre existence. These timid, inhibited, lazy souls, full of subtle forms of selfishness, are content to let the days, the years, go by sine spe nec metu (neither hoping nor fearing), without setting themselves demanding targets, nor experiencing the hopes and fears of battle: the important thing for them is to avoid the risk of disappointment and tears. How far one is from obtaining something, if the very wish to possess it has been lost through fear of the demands involved in achieving it!.*"[14] This is a kind of perverted humility. The lukewarm person does not want to accept God's graces because it would necessarily involve some duty to reciprocate, to complicate one's life. He therefore dreams up all kinds of excuses to justify his self-love: "*Insidiousness, guile, craft, and concupiscence are the refuge of small-minded and small-souled persons.*"[15]

An authentic interior life is manifested by magnanimity or high-mindedness, according to St. Thomas (*extenso animi ad magna*).[16] A person with a strong interior life will be well disposed to undertake ambitious ventures for God and for other people. This principle is corroborated by the lives of the saints. The saints provide a striking testimony to the exercise of magnanimity in the apostolate. They remind us that we should think of other people as children of God who can, with the help of God's grace, become saints.

Magnanimity is based on the virtues of humility and generosity. It springs from a profound supernatural understanding of life, in other words, from an attitude of complete trust in God. As St. Paul wrote to the Romans, "*Who*

---

[14]J. Escrivá, *Friends of God*, 207.
[15]J. Pieper, *The Four Cardinal Virtues*, p. 20.
[16]St. Thomas, *Summa Theologica*, 2-2, q. 129 e.

shall separate us from the love of Christ? Shall tribulation, or distress, or persecution, or famine, or nakedness, or peril, or sword? (...) But in all these things we overcome because of him who has loved us."[17]

"*Fearless frankness is the hallmark of high-mindedness; nothing is further from it than to suppress truth from fear. Flattery and dissimulation are equally removed from the high-minded. The high-minded man does not complain; for his heart is impervious to external evil. High-mindedness implies an unshakable firmness of hope, an actually challenging assurance, and the perfect peace of a fearless heart. The high-minded man bows neither to confusion of the soul, nor to any man, nor to fate—but to God alone.*"[18] The magnanimous person dares to aspire to greatness because he knows that "*the gift of grace raises man to things that are above his nature.*"[19] His actions, therefore, take on a divine efficacy. He becomes a participant in the power of God, who "*is able from these stones to raise up children to Abraham.*"[20] The magnanimous person is daring in the apostolate because he realizes that "*the Holy Spirit avails himself of the word of man as his instrument. But it is he (the Holy Spirit) who interiorly perfects the work.*"[21] The efficacy of the apostolate depends on God who gives the growth.[22] In marked contrast, the lukewarm person operates without a living faith. He relies on his own limited powers and is quickly disheartened. He and his efforts are essentially "small in spirit."

[17]Rom 8:35; 37.
[18]J. Pieper, *The Four Cardinal Virtues*, p. 190.
[19]St. Thomas, *Summa Theologica*, 2-2, q. 171, a. 2.
[20]Matt 3:9.
[21]St. Thomas, *Summa Theologica*, 2-2, q. 177, a. 1.
[22]Cf. 1 Cor 3:7.

Uncontrolled imagination and mental prayer

The person who has interior life is able to draw good from all the varied circumstances and events in the world. He does not wait for the dawning of certain ideal conditions for spiritual growth. He knows that these conditions exist solely in the imagination. Regrettably, this awareness is not shared by the lukewarm person. He has cut himself off from the real world and from the graces of the Holy Spirit.

The lukewarm person prefers to live in the secluded preserve of his imagination. Even though he interacts with the outside world, he interacts in a most superficial way. He frequently succumbs to external sensations and images, only to find himself impoverished as a result. He lets himself go in the things of the world. He easily becomes entangled in his own ideas and scruples. He lacks any deep convictions and bends with every wind. He receives his opinions and philosophy of life from the media. He is quite reluctant to meditate on the hollow nature of his interior life.

The lukewarm person becomes incapable of seeing any beauty or joy in ordinary life. His sadness is rooted in his very self. St. Thomas calls this uneasy restlessness of the mind *"evagatio mentis."* Since *"no one can remain in sadness,"*[23] the lukewarm person attempts to escape from himself and from reality. In the course of his daily affairs, he will take refuge in fantastic dreams. He will allow his imagination to go more and more out of control. These fantasies will often be the occasion for impurity. When a person inhabits his imagination in this way, friendship with Our Lord is practically impossible. *"For its part, evagatio mentis reveals itself in loquaciousness (verbositas), in excessive curiosity (curiositas), in an irreverent urge 'to pour oneself out*

[23]St. Thomas, *De Malo*, 11, 4.

from the peak of the mind onto many things' (importunitas), in interior restlessness (inquietudo), and in instability of place or purpose (instabilitas loci vel propositi)."[24]

The third daughter of lukewarmness, *mental torpor and sloth,* is intimately related to this restless condition. It is an inability to progress in love for God. This problem is most evident when the person goes to pray. (This seems like a waste of time.) The same difficulty may arise with respect to reading the Holy Gospel or some spiritual book. (I don't get anything out of it.) Little by little, the interior life appears ever more unattainable until that moment when it is denied. This attitude of pragmatism is the product of our secularized times wherein God has been relegated to the sidelines. We see many Christians today who appear to have been won over by the spirit of the age. They have put aside the fact of their Baptism and their religious education. They have allowed their piety to be corrupted by the paganism in our environment. Whatever remains of their faith is not strong enough to have a decisive influence on their lives and surroundings. These people appear to have lost their ability to pray.

Resentment and wickedness

The lukewarm person has no mooring in objective reality. He is at the mercy of his unrestrained feelings and inner drives. This means he is at war with himself. The lukewarm person will attempt to justify his infidelity by blaming other people or external forces. He may even draw up a list.

Who or what might be held responsible? The people he lives with, the place where he lives, his superiors or sub-

[24]J. Pieper, *On Hope,* p. 58.

ordinates, perhaps some little sickness... In sum, he will blame everyone and everything but himself. And he will continue to move further and further away from the Lord. *"Although he really should react otherwise, he becomes indignant at the failings of others. He considers their defects to be incorrigible, as opposed to correctable errors that can be overcome with the help of God's grace. What makes the lukewarm person most uncomfortable, however, are the virtues that he sees in others. These virtues are like slaps on his face. He does not hesitate to disparage virtuous people as fanatics. Along a similar vein, the lukewarm person can become quite annoyed by apostolic activities. For people are being encouraged to embrace a state which the lukewarm person has not been faithful to. This is most exasperating to the lukewarm person."*[25]

It is in this way that resentment is born and nurtured. The lukewarm person can show himself to be quite ferocious against activities that merit his respect and love. He sets himself as a judge so as to root out whatever is negative. His zeal to correct others, though, is not matched by a zeal to correct himself. *"It almost seems as though some people are now wearing glasses that disfigure their vision. In principle, they reject the possibility of a virtuous life or, at least, the constant effort to do the right thing. Everything they take in is colored by their own previous deformation. For them, even the most noble and unselfish actions are only hypocritical contortions designed to appear good. 'When they clearly discover goodness,' writes St. Gregory the Great, 'they scrutinize it in the hope of finding hidden defects' (Morals, 6, 22)."*

When such a deformation has become almost second nature it is difficult to help people to see that it is both more human and more truthful to think well of others. St. Augustine recommends the following rule-of-thumb: *"Try to acquire the virtues you believe lacking in your brothers. Then*

---

[25]J. M. Pero-Sanz, *The Church in Time of Crisis*, p. 59.

you will no longer see their defects, for you will no longer have them yourselves.' Some would find this way of acting naive. They are wiser, more 'realistic.' "[26]

Thus, resentment and critical spirit can degenerate into a veritable *odium religionis*: an irrational and satanic hatred for anything that has to do with God.[27]

It is of the essence of good judgment that all the relevant facts be considered. It is also important that the person who judges have a proper interior disposition. Every judgment is in some way "colored" by the inclinations of the person involved. The proud or envious person will always inject personal bitterness into his criticism. The lukewarm person is not well disposed to pass judgment on others. He put into his criticism the sadness and discord which envelop his soul. *"For, if criticism is to be just, constructive, effective and sanctifying, you need to love other people, you need to love your neighbor. If you in fact do love them then any criticism you make is always an act of virtue and a positive help to the person you address: 'A brother helped by his brother has the strength of a walled city' (Prov 18:19)."*[28] Because the faith of the lukewarm is asleep, his charity is cold. He will judge with the measure of his own sadness.

[26]J. Escrivá, *Christ is Passing By*, 67-68.
[27]St. Thomas, *Summa Theologica*, 2-2, q. 34, a. 6; q. 158, a. 7 ad 2.
[28]S. Canals, *Jesus as Friend*, p. 64.

VIII

VENIAL SIN

Tolerance of venial sin

"As we walk along it is inevitable that we will raise dust; we are creatures and full of defects. I would almost say that we will always need defects. They are the shadow which shows up the light of God's grace and our resolve to respond to God's kindness. And this chiaroscuro will make us human, humble, understanding and generous."[1]

The Lord has taken our sins and defects into account. He is well aware of our weakness and is willing to come to our aide at a moment's notice. The largesse of the Lord's mercy, however, should not be a motive for complacency on our part. The person who tolerates venial sins has signed a death warrant on his interior life. *"Venial sins do great harm to the soul. That's why Our Lord says in the Canticle of Canticles—Capite nobis vulpes parvulas, quae demoliuntur vineas— Catch the little foxes that destroy the vines."*[2]

A person does not fall into the state of lukewarmness because of any one particular defeat. A person becomes

[1] J. Escrivá, *Christ is Passing By*, 76.
[2] J. Escrivá, *The Way*, 329.

lukewarm as a result of a gradual acceptance of sin. Our progress or regress in the interior life will depend to a large extent on our attitude towards venial sin.

Certainly there is no doubt that mortal sin represents man's greatest misfortune. *"Don't forget, my son, that for you there is but one evil on earth: sin. You must fear it and avoid it with the grace of God."*[3] No misfortune can compare with mortal sin: neither the loss of one's fortune or one's honor, nor the most painful infirmity. The state of mortal sin brings with it the loss of sanctifying grace and all divine gifts, as well as the benefits derived from our past merits. The worst thing that can happen to the soul after mortal sin is venial sin.

A key difference between mortal sin and venial sin is the disposition of the person involved. *"For venial sin does not deprive one wholly of the life of grace and of friendship with God; it is not a conscious and free decision to do what is gravely wrong. Venial sin is a less serious offense against the law of God... No human action, however evil it might appear to be, can be a mortal sin in the strict formal sense, with all the grave consequences that implies, unless the action is done with an awareness that it is evil and a willingness to do it despite that."*[4]

Consequences of venial sin

A person who has become accustomed to venial sin is a person who has fallen out of love. *"It is not a turning away from God, but a shortcoming, a hesitation or misstep as it were, in one's efforts to follow after Christ."*[5] This sad state brings with it the loss of many graces from the Holy Spirit. It means that we have lost a priceless treasure.

[3]*Ibid.*, 386.
[4]R. Lawler et al., ed., *The Teaching of Christ*, p. 306.
[5]R. Lawler et al., ed., *Ibid.*, p. 307.

Venial sin has the effect of diminishing the fervor of our charity. It chains us down to spiritual mediocrity. Venial sin weighs down our progress in the interior life. The Blessed Josemaría Escrivá has written: *"How sad you make me feel when you are not sorry for your venial sins! For, until you are, you cannot begin to have true interior life."*[6] Venial sin makes it harder for us to practice the virtues. We begin to fear that spiritual progress is hopelessly difficult, even irksome. Perhaps worst of all, venial sin predisposes a person to mortal sin.

Venial sin makes a person insensitive to things divine. It is, in this respect, dehumanizing. Something similar occurs when a person goes to a concert but has no capacity to appreciate the music that is performed. Another example would be the person who looks upon a great work of art and can only think of asking, "What does this cost?" The person who accepts venial sin disqualifies himself, little by little, from the life of God. But he does disqualify himself. He becomes alienated from his reason for being, which is "to know, love and serve God."

In the next life, venial sins will need to be cleansed in Purgatory. We could have avoided this necessity if only we had made a little more effort during our time on earth. Venial sin also prevents a greater increase of glory for all eternity. This means that we will be giving less glory to God than we otherwise could have.

The fight against venial sins

We must struggle against venial sins throughout our life. Without some special grace, as that which was received by the Virgin, it is impossible to remain in a habitual state

[6]J. Escrivá, *The Way*, 330.

of perfect love for God.[7] We must earnestly fight against venial sin. We must flee from temptation and make reparation for our past faults. If we were to condone our sins, we would slide inexorably into a state of lukewarmness. Without a doubt, the interior life truly begins when the soul firmly resolves to resist venial sin.

If we are to fight successfully against venial sin, we will need to avail ourselves of supernatural weapons. Mere human desire and effort will not suffice. As St. Paul reminded the first Christians of Philippi, *"For God is at work in you, both to will and to work for his good pleasure."*[8]

The very desire to combat sin is dependent on the grace of God. We must be determined to ask God for a greater sensitivity to sin. He will show us the magnitude of just one venial sin. He will grant us the desire to be free from the dominion of the evil one. Let us pray for a deeper sense of sin. We do not give proper importance to how we offend God in our lack of rectitude of intention, in our uncharitable behavior, in our laziness, in our impatience, in our critical spirit, in our cold indifference to the suffering of others. How easily we forgive ourselves for inattention during our prayer or during the Mass, for surrendering to our whims, for dialoguing with temptations in the area of sensuality... *"If all these tiny faults were to be piled up on top of us, would they not crush us by their weight? What is the difference between being crushed by iron or being crushed by sand? Iron is a solid mass whereas the sand would be composed of many tiny particles. Yet in the end the effect would be the same. Venial sins! Don't you see how the mighty rivers originate in tiny droplets of water? They are miniscule but they have a great effect."*[9]

---

[7]Council of Trent, Session VI, c. 23.
[8]Phil 2:13.
[9]St. Augustine, *Sermon 56*, 12.

The Lord has promised us that whatever we ask for will be granted to us, if it is to our benefit. *"Ask, and it will be given you; seek, and you will find; knock, and it will be opened to you."*[10] We should have confidence in the Lord's promise, for he will never break his word.

The best way to counteract venial sin is to foster a personal commitment to reparation, contrition and piety. A person who is truly pious will be well defended against venial sin. And should it happen that this person succumb to venial sin, he will respond almost immediately with real contrition.

The science of the saints

Venial sins have the same effect on the soul that wounds have on the body. Even though some venial sins are more serious than others, we should have the same attitude to all of them.

In the first place, we must try to avoid them. No one in his right mind wants to cut his finger or have hand caught in a door. On the contrary, everyone seeks to avoid these injuries.

In the second place, if we should commit a venial sin, *we should have them taken care of as soon as possible.* We know that a physical wound which is not cared for will lead to more serious harm, perhaps even death. If we do not take care of these wounds, we will place our normal life and work in jeopardy. Something similar happens with the minor wounds on the soul which are the result of venial sin. If unattended, they can lead to grievous problems in the supernatural order. There are two differences which should be noted in this analogy. One difference is that while

[10]Matt 7:7-8.

physical wounds may heal of themselves, spiritual wounds do not heal with time. The soul is healed by contrition and nothing else. Another difference is that spiritual wounds have consequences in society at large. Venial sins cut us off from God and harm others in the Mystical Body of Christ. Each venial sin is a step away from friendship with Jesus Christ.

We must ask God for the grace of not losing our sense of venial sin. It is intimately related to our sense of love. We should also pray that we do not lose our sensitivity to little things and that we have sorrow over small failings.

Once we appreciate the true nature of our faults, we should be moved to sincere *contrition*. We will need God's grace if we are to be sorry for our sins. Contrition makes us forget ourselves and allows us to approach God with renewed love. Contrition always attracts God's mercy. The Lord says, *"But this is the man to whom I will look, he that is humble and contrite in spirit, and trembles at my word."*[11]

Contrition is not a matter of excusing ourselves. It may be that we are in the habit of forgiving our sins. *"Instead of acknowledging our faults, we seem more inclined to find an excuse for them. We do not want to admit that we are lazy, that we are haughty, that we are cowardly, that we are worldly or egoistic. And we find the reasons to justify our situation. Or it may happen that we do not excuse ourselves as much as we accept things with a pessimistic spirit. We say to ourselves, 'It is true. I am a coward; I am inconstant; I am a quitter; I am an egoist.' But the acknowledgment of these defects does not yield contrition, but only sadness and discouragement.*

"If we want to get out of this predicament, there is a Christian response. It is the science of repentance. We have to learn how to repent. This is what God is asking of us. We must react with faith to those negative things in ourselves or in our environment,

---

[11] Is 66:2.

thereby changing our reaction from an outlook of despair to an
outlook of hope. This is the science which has been practised by
all the saints."[12]

A point of reference

'Pardon me, I'm sorry,' is something we often say to
other people. Whenever we annoy or disturb another
person, we automatically use phrases to this effect. At times
we are expressing our inmost feelings. At other times we
are practising a polite formula which is necessary for social
harmony.

People may say 'I'm sorry' to their neighbors without
really meaning it at all. Yet when we ask for God's pardon,
we are not performing a social custom. Our hearts have to
be in our words. Our repentance has to be true and *internal*.
By all means, we should not succumb to the hypocrisy of
the scribes and the Pharisees. The Lord directed to them
perhaps his harshest rebuke: *"Woe to you, scribes and Phari-*
sees, hypocrites! For you cleanse the outside of the cup and of the
plate, but inside they are full of extortion and rapacity. You blind
Pharisee! First cleanse the inside of the cup and of the plate, that
the outside also may be clean."[13]

True sorrow for our sins does not mean that we have
to feel emotional pain. As in the case of love, sorrow is an
act of the will. It is not an outburst of emotion. Just as we
can love God without experiencing any feelings one way
or the other, so too can we have a sincere sorrow for our
sins and faults without any emotional content.

The first step in our learning how to repent is to put
ourselves in the presence of Christ, face-to-face, without

[12]A. G. Dorronsoro, *Time to Believe*, p. 136.
[13]Matt 23:25-26.

anything standing between him and us. We shall then relive Peter's moving experience following the miraculous catch of fish. *"But when Simon Peter saw it, he fell down at Jesus' knees, saying, 'Depart from me, for I am a sinful man, O Lord.' For he was astonished, and all that were with him, at the catch of fish which they had taken..."*[14]

Peter is astonished. Suddenly, everything became clear in a moment in time: the holiness of Christ and the sinfulness of man. Black is set in contrast to white; darkness, to light; filth, to cleanliness.

"Depart from me." Peter asks the Lord to go because he thinks that he is unworthy to experience the sanctity of Christ. But even as his lips say these words, his eyes reflect a humble longing for the Lord never to go away. Even though he is a poor sinner, Peter wants Christ to be his support and his point of reference. We will only understand the merit of our actions if we compare them to the love of Christ. Otherwise we shall be tempted to justify everything by our own imperfect standards.

Contrition serves to strengthen our friendship with God. It is precisely after his act of contrition that Peter learns the transcendental meaning of his life: *" 'Do not be afraid; henceforth you will be catching men.' And when they had brought their boats to land, they left everything and followed him."*

After this invitation from the Lord, Peter's life was never the same. From then on his only aims were to love Christ and to do apostolate. Everything else in his life would serve as a means to that end. It is significant that Peter's decision came in the wake of a profound act of contrition. This is why our errors should not make us discouraged. If we are humble and repentant, these errors should become occasions for a renewed encounter with

[14]Luke 5:8-9.

Christi. *" For those who love God, all things work unto good: God directs all things and events to the benefit of souls, in such a way that even those who stray or overstep their limits may move forward in virtue. This occurs when they react to mistakes by becoming more humble and experienced."*[15]

Judas and Peter

Peter knew how to repent. On a later occasion, only hours after the Last Supper, Peter openly renounced the Lord at the prompting of a mischievous servant girl. A short while afterwards, Jesus was being led to the dungeon of the high priest's palace. *"And the Lord turned and looked at Peter. And Peter remembered the word of the Lord... And he went out and wept bitterly."*[16] One glance from the Lord was enough for Peter. *"Their looks meet. Peter would like to bow his head, but he cannot tear his eyes from him, whom he has just denied. He knows the Savior's looks well; that look that had determined his vocation, he had not been able to resist either its authority or its charm; and that tender look of the Master's on the day he had affirmed, looking at his disciples, 'Here are my brethren, my sisters, my mother!' And that look that had made him tremble when, he, Simon, had wanted to banish the Cross from Jesus' path! And the affectionately pitying look with which he had invited the too-rich young man to follow him! And his look, clouded with tears, before Lazarus' tomb... He knows them well, the Savior's looks. And yet never, never had he seen on the Savior's face the expression he sees there at this moment, the eyes marked with sadness but without any severity. A look of reproach, without a doubt, but which becomes suppliant at the same time and seems to repeat to him 'Simon, I have prayed for thee!'*

[15]St. Augustine, *De correp. et prat.,* 9, 24.
[16]Luke 22:61-62.

*"This look only rests on him for an instant, Jesus was vio-
lently dragged away by the soldiers, but Peter sees him all the
time. He sees the Savior's indulgent look not weighing up but
alighting on the smarting wound of his fault."*[17]

That one look from the Lord saved Peter from despair.
It was, above all, a look of encouragement. Peter felt himself
to be understood and forgiven. How this encounter must
have reminded him of the parable of the Good Shepherd
and the lost sheep, or that of the prodigal son!

Judas also received that look of love from the Lord, that
invitation to repentance, there in the Garden of Gethse-
mane. At the very climax of betrayal, Judas heard this
salutation from Christ: *"Friend, why are you here?"*[18] Jesus
gives this same look to each one of us whenever we fall
victim to sin.

Judas received this same look in the Cenacle when the
Lord knelt down before him and washed his feet.

Judas indeed repented of his crime: *"When Judas, his
betrayer, saw that he was condemned, he repented and brought
back the thirty pieces of silver..."*[19] He repented for what he
had done, strictly speaking, but he had no hope that he
could be pardoned. He lacked the humility required to
return to Christ. He was not really sorry for having offended God.

What a tremendous difference between the behavior of
Peter and Judas! Both men had betrayed the Master, albeit
in different ways. Both men had repented. But Peter went
on to become the foundation of the Church while Judas
went and hanged himself. The repentance of Judas remained within himself. In his case, there was no conversion. The truth is that repentance alone is not enough. Mere

[17]G. Chevrot, *Simon Peter*, Sinag-tala Publishers 1984, pp. 189-190.
[18]Matt 26:50.
[19]Cf. Matt 27:3-10.

repentance will yield only anguish, bitterness and despair. On the other hand, repentance that leads to Christ brings forth a joyful sorrow because the sinner regains his friendship with the Lord. This explains how Peter was lifted up from his denials to a greater sense of union with the Lord. Thanks to Christ's assistance, Peter's denials bore fruit in a fidelity so strong that it weathered even martyrdom.

Judas remained alone. The chief priests responded to his repentance, *"What is that to us? See to it yourself."* Judas suffers from the isolation which results from sin. He does not go to Christ. He could have become one of the pillars of the Church, in spite of his betrayal, but he lacked hope. All this having been said, we do not know what transpired in the heart of that sad fellow in the last moments of his life.

Peter went out. He knew that because of his foolish imprudence he was in the wrong place. He wanted to avoid a relapse.

According to St. Augustine, this act of getting out of the courtyard *"represents the confession of sin. 'He wept bitterly' because he knew how to love. Soon enough he found that the sweetness of love supplanted the bitterness of sorrow."*[20] This is the history of every person who, after an offense, be it big or small, truly repents and weeps over his sin.

We should exercise this spirit of contrition every time something goes wrong in our life, every time we do the examination of conscience, every time we confess our sins. This is the radical cure for lukewarmness. While this sacrament is principally directed to the forgiveness of sins, it also prepares and strengthens the soul for the future, thanks to the repentance of the sinner, the absolution of the priest and the penance that is imposed. Because of the effects of this sacrament, the penitent's tendency to relapse

[20]St. Augustine, *Sermon 295*, 3.

is diminished while his disposition to do the good is fortified. The penitent may also obtain new and actual graces
to resist and avoid venial sin. All of this depends to a large
extent, however, on how well we make use of this sacrament. We should struggle to avoid any sense of routine in
this regard.

The antidote

On a certain night a wealthy and influential man, a
Pharisee, came to speak with Jesus. He had a long and
profound conversation with the Lord. St. John is the only
Evangelist who recorded the incident.[21] Perhaps he was
there present.

Nicodemus was a man of good will who saw that there
was something special in Jesus. He was one of those Jews
who was looking forward to the salvation of Israel.

In the course of their conversation, Nicodemus had the
humility to approach Jesus as a teacher. Even though
Nicodemus was a member of the Sanhedrin well advanced
in years, he was ready to learn from an itinerant preacher
from Galilee. The entire dialogue is characterized by a deep
respect. *"Rabbi, we know that you are a teacher come from
God..."* It is true that Nicodemus came by night, but he did
this as an act of prudence. He was not afraid of what people
would say, as he later demonstrated during the darkest
moments of Good Friday.

For his part, Jesus speaks to Nicodemus with the respect
due to a man of his stature and education. Jesus teaches
Nicodemus about the need for souls to be baptized if they
are to enter the Kingdom of Heaven. He reveals to this
Pharisee the nature of the Holy Spirit and the meaning of

[21]Cf. John 3:1 ff.

his salvific death. It is at this juncture that the Lord quotes a passage from the Old Testament: *"And as Moses lifted up the serpent in the wilderness, so must the Son of man be lifted up, that whoever believes in him may have eternal life."*

This passage may be found in the book of Numbers. It refers to a critical moment during the Exodus when the people of Israel became impatient about their sorry lot and started to speak against God and against Moses. *"Then the Lord sent fiery serpents among the people, and they bit the people, so that many people of Israel died. And the people came to Moses, and said, 'We have sinned, for we have spoken against the Lord and against you; pray to the Lord, that he take away the serpents from us.' So Moses prayed for the people. And the Lord said to Moses, 'Make a fiery serpent, and set it on a pole; and every one who is bitten, when he sees it, shall live.' "*[22]

Down through the centuries, the People of God journey towards the Promised Land. Throughout their travels, God's children are continually being threatened by the serpents and their venom in various manifestations: murmurings, envy, egoism, sensuality, doctrinal confusion... The baptized faithful always encounter more or less the same enemies. Just as sensuality and egoism and heresy and confusion were rampant in the Fourth Century, they were equally present in the Thirteenth Century and are equally present in the Twentieth Century. And when the Twenty-First Century arrives or, for that matter, the Twenty-Third Century, the faithful will also have to struggle with the consequences of Original Sin.

There are three things that remain constant throughout time: the serpents, their venom and the antidote. The cure will always be the same: to raise one's sights to Christ. Look at him, contemplate him, accompany him. Piety! *"And as Moses lifted up the serpent in the wilderness, so must the Son*

[22]Num 21:6-8.

of man be lifted up, that whoever believes in him may have eternal life."

"For God so loved the world that he gave his only Son, that whoever believes in him should not perish but have eternal life."[23]

Piety. If we truly want to reach the Promised Land, that everlasting reward for our efforts during a short time on earth, then we must not lose sight of Christ.

Let us not lose sight of Christ just because we see all around us the ravages wrought by the enemy. Truly, no one is immune if they rely on solely their own forces. The antidote for our faults and failings has a supernatural origin. We have to seek it in personal prayer, in the Sacraments, in an ever-increasing friendship with the Lord.

Imagine for a moment a large building which has many cracks and crevices. The cold wind enters into the building through these holes. One could go about the building trying to seal these many cracks, but it would probably be smarter to first get a fire going inside. Then you could go around plugging up the problem areas one by one, starting with the bigger ones. This fire should be thought of as our love for Christ. It must be fed by our childlike and sincere piety, by our frequent conversation with the Lord. The Blessed Josemaría Escrivá has given this pertinent advice: *"Try to commit yourself to a plan of life and keep to it: a few minutes of mental prayer, Holy Mass—daily, if you can manage it—and frequent Communion; regular recourse to the Holy Sacrament of Forgiveness—even though your conscience does not accuse you of mortal sin; visiting Jesus in the Tabernacle; praying and contemplating the mysteries of the Holy Rosary, and so many other marvellous devotions you know or can learn.*

"You should not let them become rigid rules, or water-tight compartments. They should be flexible, to help you on your journey you who live in the middle of the world, with a life of

[23]John 3:14-16.

hard professional work and social ties and obligations which you should not neglect, because in them your conversation with God still continues. Your plan of life ought to be like a rubber glove which fits the hand perfectly.

"Please don't forget that the important thing does not lie in doing many things; limit yourself, generously, to those you can fulfill each day, whether or not you happen to feel like doing them. These pious practices will lead you, almost without your realizing it, to contemplative prayer. Your soul will pour forth more acts of love, aspirations, acts of thanksgiving, acts of atonement, spiritual communions. And this will happen while you go about your ordinary duties, when you answer the telephone, get on a bus, open or close a door, pass in front of a church, when you begin a new task, during it and when you have finished it: you will find yourself referring everything you do to your Father God."[24] We will then discover that our friendship with God is the best protection against even the strongest of temptations.

Increasing the pressure

There was once a certain overland train line that had a lot of problems because of the wind. The wind was constant, dry, usually full of sand and dust. The train company did all that it could to protect the passengers: improved seals in the cars, double-plated glass, etc. In spite of all these efforts, the passengers would invariably arrive at their destination covered with a film of dust. After a good deal of study and experimentation, somebody came up with a bright idea: increase the interior pressure of the cabins. The problem was solved overnight.

Something similar may be observed with regard to our interior life. There is a great wind of polluted air circulating

[24] J. Escrivá, *Friends of God*, 149.

about us. Even if we do our best to avoid its effects, our soul can become soiled. The best way for us to protect ourselves is through a life of true piety. As a consequence, many of our problems will no longer be problems of any significance. If we strive to be more in the presence of God, we will keep out the dust.

A person who lives the virtue of piety sees other people, things and events in a supernatural way. The action of grace gives a wonderful 'naturalness' and strength to the soul. Grace helps us to go around the puddles of venial sin that lie scattered along our path.

IX

LOVE FOR FREQUENT CONFESSION

Who will repair us?

The story is told of a poor violinist who struggled to make a living by playing in the streets. He would travel from town to town. When he would begin to play, the crowds would gather and he would pass his cap around in search of their spare change.

One fine day he began to play as usual and the people stopped to listen. The music was more or less harmonious. Neither the violin nor the violinist had anything more to give.

Then a famous composer passed by who was a violin virtuoso. He joined the crowd and at the conclusion of the performance he took the violin into his hands. He tuned the instrument and then played a marvellous piece which left everyone astounded. The owner was amazed and he walked about the composer saying to himself in disbelief, *"That is my violin!"* The wandering violinist never dreamed that his old strings had such potential.

With a little bit of examination of conscience, we can see ourselves as that underutilized violin. We are poor instruments that are frequently out of tune.

Whenever we attempt anything serious in life, the result is noise, discordance. If we should end up being successful, then we feel compelled to pass our cap around for applause, respect, praise... This is what keeps us going. And if the people around us don't appreciate our work, then we feel cheated. We fall victim to pessimism and self-pity. In this way we give life to that old refrain: *"He who lives on crumbs is always hungry."* We are never satisfied.

But what a difference there is when we allow God to repair us, to tune us up! What a difference when we let God play as he wills! Then we become instruments of God. Then we find ourselves amazed at our incredible potential. Our life is simply magnificent when we allow ourselves to be instruments of the Lord. Truly, only God can satisfy our deepest longings.

Jesus is the only one who can repair our life. Only he can get the most out of his violins. He is our *Teacher*. He shows us the way that leads to joy and salvation. We can trust him completely, since he teaches with authority.[1]

He is our *Physician*. He knows everything there is to know about what is wrong with the world and what the best remedies are. As far as Christ is concerned, there is no such thing as an incurable disease. He can solve our every problem. All we have to do is go to him with confidence and docility. *"He is our physician, and he heals our selfishness, if we let his grace penetrate to the depths of our soul. Jesus has taught us that the worst sickness is hypocrisy, the pride that leads us to hide our own sins. We have to be totally sincere with him. 'Lord, if you will'—and you are always willing—'you can make me clean'. You know my weaknesses; I feel these symptoms; I suffer from these failings. We show him the wound, with simplicity, and if the wound is festering, we show the pus too. Lord, you have cured so many souls; help me to recognize you as the divine*

---

[1]Cf. Matt 7:29.

physician, when I have you in my heart or when I contemplate your presence in the Tabernacle."[2]

And when at times we feel really sick, let us take consolation in those moving words of Jesus: *"Those who are well have no need of a physician, but those who are sick.*"[3] It is in these trials that the Lord is closer to us than ever before... no matter how badly we have fallen, no matter how often, no matter how unforgivable it seems to us.

When it comes right down to it, we all are a bit sick. As a consequence, we all are in need of Christ. He is the cure for every one of our ills.

Jesus is our Friend, *"that great friend, who will never fail you.*"[4] He is always ready to give us a hand, to comfort us, to encourage us. If we live with Christ, we will never be alone. He has wanted to become man so that we might go to him without fear. And he is the same God who can do anything.

Jesus is the Good Shepherd who looks for his lost sheep. He carries it on his shoulders back to the flock. Whenever we lose our way, Christ goes out to look for us. He is ready to bestow every conceivable grace and gift upon us, that is, if we let him. Every single one of us is extremely precious to him.

Jesus knows each sheep by name. He defends them and guides them to safe and abundant pastures. The Psalmist proclaims, *"The Lord is my shepherd, I shall not want... Even though I walk through the valley of the shadow of death, I fear no evil; for thou art with me; thy rod and thy staff, they comfort me.*"[5]

Sometimes he acts directly on the soul, at other times through the sacraments, those channels of grace. He may

[2]J. Escrivá, *Christ is Passing By,* 93.
[3]Matt 9:12.
[4]Cf. J. Escrivá, *The Way,* 88.
[5]Ps 22:1-4.

also act through the agency of other persons, events, etc.
But it is in the Sacrament of Penance that the Lord restores
us to the life of grace. This Sacrament has been instituted
thanks to the mercy of God for the forgiveness of sins and
faults. It is here that we can have the assurance of God's
loving pardon. Every time we confess our sins, we can
resume our life with a cheerful attitude. This is because we
have personally experienced the fact that God is ready to
forgive us our every sin. He has his arms wide open for his
mercy is infinite.

Frequent confession helps us to become better instruments, even though our past faults and sins may have been
many in number. It is in this Sacrament that the Lord
repairs and tunes his violins.

Frequent Confession and the fight against lukewarmness

Lukewarmness takes root wherever the terrain permits.
It is to be found in the company of carelessness, negligence
and venial sin. Usually these faults do not amount to
important things, at least individually. They involve little
concessions related to whims, habitual intemperance,
uncorrected character flaws, tardiness, excessive worries
about money or about the future, attachments to things or
persons, etc. These small concessions can dispose the soul
towards mortal sin. These minor faults are always fertile
ground for the growth of lukewarmness in the soul. *"While
it is quite normal that everyone will sin in small matters,"* says
St. Augustine, *"no one should treat these sins casually. How
true it is that many small offences can add up to something quite
sizeable. The same phenomenon may be observed in that many
small drops make up a river. So too many small pieces of dirt
constitute a mountain. In conclusion, where can we place our*

hope? *Above all other things, we should have recourse to Confession."*[6]

If we make a sincere and contrite confession of our sins, we will be freed from our sins and failings. And since we are by nature weak and prone to sin, we should practise frequent Confession. Then we will have a clean and sensitive soul. As a result, lukewarmness will not be able to take root. "In frequent Confession we have everything that will guard us against tepidity. For one thing, frequent Confession compels us to look into ourselves seriously to see our sins and faults, to elicit an act of contrition for them and formulate a purpose of amendment regarding them. In other words, it makes us apply ourselves with full deliberation and determination to improving our lives. Then, too, Confession is a sacrament and consequently through it the power of Christ himself works in us. His greatest desire in this sacrament is to fill us with his own hatred of sin and with his own zeal to glorify his Father in all things, to be completely devoted to his service and fully resigned to his holy will. Finally, of considerable value is the direction we get from our confessor, who in every Confession will urge us anew and encourage us to continue along the way of virtue with full fervor."

"One of the principal reasons for esteeming frequent Confession highly is that, when practised as it should be, it is an infallible safeguard against tepidity. Perhaps it is this conviction that makes the Church recommend so strongly, indeed prescribe as an obligation, frequent or weekly Confession for clerics and religious. Therefore let us consider frequent Confession as something important and holy. And let us endeavor always to make our Confessions well, indeed to try and make them better and better every time."[7]

[6]St. Augustine, *Epistle to Parthos*, 1, 6.
[7]B. Baur, *Frequent Confession*, p. 118.

"Take heart, my son; your sins are forgiven."[8] These were Jesus' words to the paralytic. He had been brought to Jesus for a physical cure and he had been given something much greater. He had been cleansed of all his sins. Perhaps he first looked at Jesus with some fear. Yet he ended up looking at Him with boundless gratitude.

Christ repeats these same words after every good Confession: *"Take heart, your sins are forgiven."* He encourages us to begin again.

The Sacrament of Penance confers grace—or increases it when the recipient is in the state of grace—*ex opere operatio*, with an unfailing and limitless capacity all its own. Nevertheless, the effect of this Sacrament does depend upon the disposition of the penitent. We might make an analogy here to the sun which warms some things more than others, even though it is always the same sun. For one thing, the effects of the sun vary according to the season of the year. In addition, there are any number of obstacles which can block or diminish the sun's light and warmth, no matter what season it is.

A good Confession

Classical spiritual authors have handed down to us sixteen characteristics of a good Confession: simple, humble, pure, faithful, frequent, clear, discrete, voluntary, without boasting, integral, secret, sorrowful, prompt, firm, self-accusatory, disposing one to obedience.[9] Normally, our confessions should be concise. We should say what has to be said without becoming unduly wordy. More than anything else, *our confessions have to be done with a supernatu-*

[8]Matt 9:2.
[9]Cf. St. Thomas, *Summa Theologica*, Supplement, 9, 4.

ral spirit. We are asking Christ himself to forgive us our sins. This attitude will help us to put aside that temptation concerning what the priest will think of me. If our confession is truly supernatural, then we will hear Christ say to us those words he once spoke to St. Peter, *"Simon, son of John, do you love me?"* And then we will echo the Apostle's wholehearted reply, *"Domine, tu omnia nosti, tu scis quia amo te. Lord, you know everything; you know that I love you."*[10] Lord, you know that sometimes I am a failure, but you know that I love you in spite of all my infidelities.

We must do our best to avoid impersonal Confessions, ones that are vague, wordy and full of generalities. This kind of Confession usually masks self-love, a yearning to cover-up humiliations. Let us confess in a concrete and personal manner: *"I accuse myself..."* Confession is not meant to be a human dialogue or 'rap session.' It is a sacramental forum where we accuse ourselves before God himself.

Let us take care to flee from the "dumb devil." He is always lying in wait for us. If we are to be really sincere, we need to make a serious examination of conscience, if at all possible, before the Tabernacle. In any event, we should always examine ourselves in the presence of God. There is a big difference between examination of conscience in the presence of God and examination of conscience in front of, say, the mirror. By ourselves, we will tend to find excuses for our misconduct. In contrast, when we do this examination before Christ, our actions will take on their true dimension. The soul will be filled with peace and joy, even in the sad case of serious falls. True sincerity will lead us to make a *complete* confession of our sins without omitting anything because of pride or embarrassment.

We should confess our sins in *clear and concise terms*. A Confession characterized by clarity might be summarized

<hr />

[10]John 21:17-18.

in these words: *"I have sinned against heaven and before you."*
If we make our confession *with humility*, we will be freed
from worries about 'looking good.' We will speak to the
Lord without expecting anything in return: *"I am no longer
worthy to be called your son."*[11]

Confession should make us happy. Our Father God is
awaiting us with open arms just like in the parable about
the prodigal son. He is ready to run right up to us to prove
his infinite paternal love.

Confession is *followed by true repentance.* Through this
sacrament, we recover our sense of hope. Thanks to God's
healing graces, we can see once again. As a consequence,
we can make reparation for our sin and rise out of it: *"I will
arise and go to my father."* So said the prodigal son once he
finally repented of his sinful ways. Every Confession
involves a conversion, a turning towards Christ with
renewed dedication. This takes place regardless of the
severity of the offense.

In our contrition, we must do everything possible to
avoid giving into a sense of routine.

We will draw forth from our Confession a *firm and
concrete resolve to sin no more.* This involves whatever
matters may seriously jeopardize our friendship with the
Lord as well as those 'minor' infidelities which might
incline us toward lukewarmness.

Let us not be surprised by the fact that we ask God's
pardon for *the same sins and failings* over and over again.
"Observe how sea water filters into the cracks of a ship's hull,"
counsels St. Augustine, *"and little by little enters the vessel
until it is at risk of sinking. Do then as the sailors do in this
predicament: bail out the water until the hull is dry once more...
Of course, the ship will be filled with water again because the
cracks in the hull have not been stopped up. In like manner, the*

[11]Luke 15:18-19.

*cracks of human frailty will always endanger our progress. Time
and time again, we must set to work to bail out the sea water.*"[12]
There are many, many obstacles to our sanctification which
we cannot expect to vanquish at a single stroke. It is
imperative that we develop a habitual willingness to
struggle for sanctity. This is one very good reason for the
practice of frequent Confession.

"*Because of Original Sin and our own personal sins, we are
everyone of us in a state of convalescence until we die and go to
Heaven. Every person who is recovering from an illness or an
operation needs to be totally disposed to the wishes of his physician. How lucky we are to have this divine remedy of Penance
so close at hand!*"[13]

In the long history of the Church there have been
saints who went to confession on a daily basis. They were
not acting because of undue scruples and anxiety but
because they had a tremendous desire to be united with
the Lord. They knew that a humble and contrite Confession is a most efficacious means for progress in the interior
life.

One of the surest signs of real love for God is a refined
love for frequent Confession. Contrariwise, a tell-tale sign
of indifference towards God and the supernatural life is
contempt for this sacrament. "*Frequent Confession obliges us
to set to work earnestly to overcome deliberate venial sin. This
must be our attitude and our unshakable determination, if God
gives us the grace to practise frequent Confession. And, on the
other hand, it is clear that the best proof that our frequent
Confessions are well made and fruitful is that they confirm us
ever more in our resolve to eradicate venial sin from our lives.
Our faithful and laborious striving to overcome deliberate venial
sins and failings of every kind is a barometer on which we can*

[12]St. Augustine, *Sermon 16*, 7.
[13]A. Rey, *The Sacrament of Penance*, Madrid 1977, p. 137.

read whether and to what degree we are making our frequent Confessions earnestly and with fruit."[14]

How often we go to Confession will be determined by the particular needs of our soul. For any person who really wants to be a saint, who wants to belong entirely to God, weekly or bi-weekly Confession is highly recommended. In the case of a person who has an overly scrupulous conscience, it might be better to lengthen the time from one Confession to another. If a person has the misfortune to succumb to mortal sin, he or she should seek out immediately the Sacrament of Life.

[14]B. Baur, *Frequent Confession*, p. 92.

X

THE GOOD SHEPHERD

We all need spiritual direction

Confession is a sure refuge on our life's journey. There we can have all our wounds dressed and healed. We ought to keep in mind that Confession entails not only a judgment of our past sins, but also spiritual medicine. Whenever we confess our sins, we resolve to change our behavior and we dispose ourselves to spiritual direction. The confessor exercises a sacramental mission as well as a pastoral charge. His work is made a lot easier and more efficacious insofar as he knows us personally. For our part, this kind of relationship can make our Confessions more fruitful. The Blessed Josemaría Escrivá has advised us: *"If your conscience tells you that you have committed a fault—even though it does not appear to be serious or if you are in doubt— go to the Sacrament of Penance. Go to the priest who looks after you, who knows how to demand of you a steady faith, refinement of soul and true Christian fortitude. The Church allows the greatest freedom for confessing to any priest, provided he has the proper faculties; but a conscientious Christian will go—with complete freedom—to the priest he knows is a good shepherd, who*

*can help him to look up again and see once more, on high, the
Lord's star."*[1]

What great progress can be made in the interior life
when spiritual direction is combined with a good Confession! This is why we should regularly confess with a priest
who knows our soul and its struggles. Then we will be
rewarded with greater lights from God, along with an
increase in strength. We will be better able to combat our
evil inclinations as we grow in interior purity.

A spiritual director is someone who knows the ways of
God. We open our soul to him. He is our teacher, physician,
friend and good shepherd in whatever relates to God and
the supernatural life. He warns us of the obstacles we may
encounter. He suggests goals for our interior life that are
concrete and attainable. He always encourages us. Our
spiritual director helps us to discover new, unsuspected
horizons. He awakens in our soul a hunger and thirst for
God that should override any temptation to lukewarmness.

Spiritual direction serves to channel our desires for
sanctity, our efforts to overcome spiritual mediocrity, our
life-long battle against sin. This spiritual means is helpful
to the extent that we sincerely want to improve. From the
first centuries of her existence on earth, the Church has
continuously recommended that the faithful receive spiritual direction as a most efficacious instrument of spiritual
growth.

We develop in the interior life on a day by day basis.
We need to have concrete goals. There are times when we
lose our way, when our orientation becomes vague, diffuse
and inoperative.

Ordinarily, no one can guide himself without special
help from God. We are afflicted by a lack of objectivity,
by our pride, by our laziness. All of these defects have a

---

[1] J. Escrivá, *Christ is Passing By*, 34.

way of beclouding our path to God (It seemed so clear at the start!). When we enter into this state of confusion, then we are threatened with spiritual mediocrity, discouragement and lukewarmness. In marked contrast, *"a ship with a good helmsman reaches the port without danger,"* teaches St. John Climacus, *"With God's help, our spiritual director will help us to achieve our goals, even if we should stray along the way."*

Let us not imitate that young motorcyclist who was speeding along until he had to slam on the brakes to avoid hitting a professor. This close call left the professor on the ground. Once he had straightened up, he asked the young cyclist, *"Young man, where are you going?"* And the young man replied, *"I don't know, but I'm in a hurry."* Isn't this the answer which most people would give to any serious query about the meaning of their life? *"I don't know where I'm going, but I'm in a big hurry."*

If someone were to stop us in the street and ask, *"Where are you going in your life?"* How would you respond? Wouldn't it be great if we could say in all sincerity, *I am on my way to God.* I'm headed for God despite my many defects. I'm going to God through my professional work, through my family life, through the development of my character, through the perfection of my talents. I'm doing my best to get to God in spite of my weaknesses and mistakes. I know the way to go because I allow myself to be helped.

Strong friends

"Such being the penury of the times in which we live, God needs strong friends to sustain the weak."

St. Teresa

A good spiritual director is a great gift from God. What a joy to have someone to whom we can open our hearts without fear! How wonderful it is to be guided on our journey towards God! The spiritual director enjoys a special grace from God to help us. He understands our struggle and respects our efforts to improve. He encourages us and sustains us with his prayer.

It is of the utmost importance, therefore, that we select the right person to be our spiritual director. We have to make this choice with naturalness and a refined supernatural outlook. In the case of Paul, the charge fell to Ananias. He restored Paul's sight and strengthened him in his new vocation. In the case of Tobias, the task was carried out by the archangel Raphael. He took on a human form to guide Tobias on a long and difficult journey. The Virgin chose her cousin Elizabeth to be the one to reveal something of God's intentions for her. Our Lady was not acting according to human criterion in this matter for she might otherwise have elected St. Joseph. The Virgin chose Elizabeth because the angel had indicated this person in the course of his message.

In St. Luke's Gospel, Christ tells how the prodigal son was so weighed down by his sins that he felt a pressing need to unload that weight. Judas also felt weighed down by the guilt of his awful betrayal. The prodigal son knew how to return to his father for forgiveness and welcome. His repentance resulted in, of all things, a feast. Judas should have returned to Jesus for forgiveness. He would have received the same warm embrace that was extended to Simon Peter. Instead, Judas went to those who had no capacity to understand him or forgive his offense: the chief priests. They rebuked him harshly, *"What is that to us? See to it yourself."*

This question of prudent selection is reflected in ordinary life. When we get sick we go to a doctor who knows us and is able to cure our affliction. We don't go to just any old doctor. If necessary, we go to a specialist. If we have a legal problem we go to a lawyer. If we need to have our shoes repaired, we go to the nearest cobbler. If we are in Barcelona and we want to go to Granada, we check out the maps for Spain and not those for France.

If we really want to be united with God we will use the same common sense. We will allow ourselves to be guided by someone who knows the right way. If our soul is sick we don't see a medical doctor or a lawyer or a psychologist or a shoe repair man. The only person who can cure us is the person who has the grace of state to do so.

We are all well aware of our human frailty. *"Everyone knows that you need a guide to climb up a mountain. The same truth applies to the spiritual ascent... This assistance is especially important because we have to avoid the many snares set by the devil who earnestly desires to impede our progress."*[2]

Spiritual direction is indispensable if we are to make real progress in the interior life. Without this guidance, we might share the sense of exasperation of the Jews who wandered aimlessly in the desert for forty years.[3] We may have lived without knowing where we are going. God may not have held a central role in our work, study, family life, etc. We may not have ordered our temporal affairs to their supernatural end, that being, sanctity and salvation. We may have lived in just any old manner, without meaning, amusing ourselves with ephemeral realities. All of these problems are rooted in the lack of spiritual guidance and concrete, personal goals.

[2]R. Garrigou-Lagrange, *The Three Ages of the Interior Life*, I, p. 297.
[3]Cf. Deut 2:1.

Woe to him who is alone!

We all need a word of encouragement once in a while. Otherwise, discouragement may seep in to our attitude. Every one of us can become discouraged from time to time. How welcome is that friendly voice which spurs us onward: *"Forward! You can do it! Don't give up because you have the grace of God to overcome any obstacle!"* The Holy Spirit speaks to us, *"For if they fall, one will lift up his fellow; but woe to him who is alone when he falls and has not another to lift him up."*[4]

With this help we are made whole once more. We can then draw increased strength even though it may seem that we have no strength left. We can press ahead. As St Augustine says, *"In the same manner that a blind man cannot follow the right way without a guide neither can anyone walk (along the way to God) without guidance."*[5]

We need spiritual direction because there are days when we cannot make out the road. We wander in the darkness. We get lost. This is when it becomes imperative that we ask another person for directions, someone who knows how to get to God. Why is this so?

—Because by ourselves we can see only external realities. We are not equipped to judge the interior world or what is best for us. Unless we know ourselves and our defects, how will we know what to struggle against? If we do not struggle, we will not advance in the spiritual life.

—Because our vision can be clouded by pride, arrogance, laziness, sensuality and the rest of the passions. We need to know the truth with as much clarity as possible. Something similar happens to a person who has been cooped up in a room for an extended period of time: the

[4]Eccles 4:10.
[5]St. Augustine, *Sermon 112.*

poor fellow gets used to the stale air. If anybody were to enter the room they would, of course, notice that problem immediately.

—Because *"your own spirit is a bad advisor, a poor pilot to steer your soul through the squalls and storms and across the reefs of the interior life. That's why it is the Will of God that the command of the ship be entrusted to a master who, with his light and knowledge, can guide us to a safe port."*[6]

—Because we are bound to sustain wounds in the spiritual combat. Some of them will be serious, requiring the attention of a specialist. Some wounds will require time to heal and close observation. In these cases, we cannot depend on just any physician we come across.

—Because God expects abundant fruits from us. Abundant fruits, because his graces have been abundant. We are continually menaced by the threat of lukewarmness, the danger of our not being generous to God in family life, at work, in the varied circumstances of our life.

We cannot fool ourselves. If we want to live in God's presence, we need the guidance of our spiritual director. Let us not fall prey to the changing fancies of our own counsel. What a shame if we would rely on our own ego, on our feelings, on the dictates of the media. We cannot expect special graces from God if we refuse to take advantage of the ordinary means which are well within our reach. St. Vincent Ferrer advises us that *"Our Lord, without whom we can do nothing, never grants his grace to one who, having access to a person who can instruct and direct him, despises this most efficacious means of sanctification, believing that he suffices unto himself, and that by his own powers he can seek and find what is necessary for his salvation... He who has a director whom he obeys without reservation and in all things, will attain his end much more easily than if he were alone, even if he were blessed*

---

[6]Cf. J. Escrivá, *The Way*, 59.

with the most awesome intelligence and the holiest books on spiritual matters..."

Water has to run along its bed. If it should become stagnated, it will usually become putrefied. St. Teresa had the habit of saying, with her typical human and supernatural wisdom, that each and every soul needs a drainage system.

XI

LOVE FOR GOD
AND OTHER PEOPLE

No one can give what he does not have

During the Second World War, one of the bombardments left a little German village almost completely destroyed. And with the town, the church. At the main altar there had hung a life-size image of Christ crucified, to which the people of that district were very devoted. Following that bombardment, the local people found the corpus amidst the debris but without its arms.

When the time for reconstruction came, the people could not agree on what to do with their beloved image. Some wanted to install new arms on the body. Others were inclined to make a replica of the crucifix as it once had been. In the end, after much discussion, the congregation decided to use the damaged corpus without replacing the arms. Instead, they put up the following inscription: *You are my arms...* This is how the crucifix stands on the back altarpiece of that church to this very day.

We are the arms of God in the world. He has wanted to remain in the Tabernacle so that we may go to him, listen to him, draw strength from him. He gives us the charge of spreading his message and his doctrine to all men and women. If we don't carry out this apostolate, it probably will not be done. Jesus Christ wants us to be his instruments. But how are we to be instruments of the Lord if we do not have supernatural life, if we are not striving for personal sanctity? *"Can a blind man lead a blind man? Will they not both fall into a pit?"*[1]

A Christian can accomplish what God expects of him only if he is determined to become a saint. We cannot forget that *"no one gives what he does not have."* Good fruit can only be gathered from the good tree.[2] And the tree is good when good sap runs through it—that means the life of Christ. Consequently, we must never become separated from him. *"He who abides in me, and I in him, he it is that bears much fruit, for apart from me you can do nothing."*[3] Through our friendship with Christ we learn how to be effective, to be joyful, to be understanding, to be strong, to be truly concerned about the others. This is how we learn to be good Christians.

We sometimes come across friends, colleagues, members of our own family, who seem to walk through life as if they were blind. They appear to have lost their way. They look to us to lead them back to God. Let us not make this a case of the blind leading the blind. If we are to help others progress, we need more than a vague and superficial knowledge of the way. It is necessary that we walk the path ourselves. We have to get to know the route and the difficulties which may crop up. In short, we need to have interior life. We need to have a vibrant friendship with Jesus. Let us resolve to get to know him better. Then we will be able to renew the struggle against our defects.

[1]Luke 6:39.
[2]Cf. Matt 7:18.
[3]John 15:5.

The apostolate is born out of love for Christ. He is the Light that we have to shine forth, the Truth that we have to teach, the Life that we have to impart.

Neutrality is impossible

"You lack drive. That's why you sway so few."[4]

We can be a cause of joy or a cause of sadness. We can be a source of light or a source of darkness. We can be a fount of peace or one of turmoil, a leaven or a dead weight that slows down the progress of others. Clearly, our behavior on this earth has consequences. Either we help others find Christ or we lead them away from him. We can either enrich or impoverish. Neutrality is impossible.

The Lord is continually asking us to bring those around us to salvation, to joy, to generosity. This task is impossible if we are lukewarm in spirit. It would be like asking a paralytic to run in a marathon.

The apostolate does not depend so much on the qualities of a person (talent, charm, good communication skills...) but on his love for God our Lord.

We may recall that before Jesus gave Peter his solemn charge of leading the Church he asked the Apostle three times, *"Simon, son of John, do you love me more than these?"* Proselytism is the fruit of love, of that unique conviction which love generates. We know that only he who is convinced can really convince others. This principle may be seen at work when we speak with God before we speak about him to somebody else. *"It is necessary that you be a 'man of God,' a man of interior life, a man of prayer and of sacrifice. Your apostolate must be the overflow of your life 'within.'"*[5]

---

[4]Cf. J. Escrivá, *The Way*, 791.
[5]J. Escrivá, *The Way*, 961.

And so, the words of the Lord are fulfilled: *"For apart from me you can do nothing."*[6] With Christ we can do anything. We can convince the others despite the most adverse environment imaginable, even in the midst of great tribulations. The history of the Church is a marvellous example for our edification. As St. John Chrysostom exhorted the first Christians, *"Do not lose heart. For even though you may be threatened with dangers from all sides, this should not extinguish your fervor..."*[7] These believers succeeded in spreading the faith to the Roman senate, to the military, to the Imperial Palace household... *"We began only yesterday and we have already filled the earth: cities and households, fortresses and townships and hamlets, even unto far-off encampments and tribes and militia, the court and the senate and the forum."*[8] Without any resources whatsoever, the first Christians converted a pagan world that had given precious little indication of interest in the supernatural life.

What has happened to the Christians of our time? At times we give the impression that we can convince only a few. The faith continues to be the same. Christ lives in our midst now as before. *"The hand of God the Lord has not grown weaker!"*[9] Is it possible that entire nations could sink into lukewarmness? Whole peoples are seen to adopt pagan customs and life-styles which are incompatible with Christianity. *"Only the tepidity of many thousands and millions of Christians can explain why so many heresies and barbaric customs could become rampant in the world. Lukewarmness vitiates the strength of the faith. It is the friend of complacency on both an individual and collective basis."*[10] The fact that faith

---

[6]John 15:5.
[7]St. John Chrysostom, *Homilies on St. Matthew's Gospel*, 46, 3.
[8]Tertullian, *Apology*, 37.
[9]Cf. J. Escrivá, *The Way*, 586.
[10]P. Rodriguez, *Faith and Life of Faith*, p. 142.

and love have been extinguished in numerous souls explains a good many of our contemporary problems. In the early days of Christianity, the 'model Christian' was the martyr and the saint. Today, in many places, the 'model Christian' is someone who is lukewarm and mediocre.

When love becomes cold and faith weakens then the leaven is turned into a lump. *"If leaven is not used for fermenting, it rots. There are two ways leaven can disappear, either by giving life to dough, or by being wasted, a perfect tribute to selfishness and barrenness."*[11] Then the leaven loses its powerful strength and becomes good for nothing.

Lukewarmness is frequently the cause of sterility in the apostolate. Although the lukewarm person may go through the motions of doing apostolate, he acts without a supernatural spirit. No one will be attracted to friendship with Christ by the example of a dead faith and empty love. The lukewarm Christian may be likened to an insect which has become entangled in a spider's web. The web is as strong as it is invisible. The insect is able to move less and less as the spider patiently prepares for its supper. The lukewarm person allows himself to become entrapped by his laziness and self-love. He becomes increasingly unable to lead others to Christ. In the end, the lukewarm person becomes apostolically sterile and wholly wrapped up in himself.

The purpose of the leaven is to transform the dough, to change it from within. If it does not serve this purpose it has ceased to be leaven. It is just another bit of dough.

A train rusting on a siding

A lack of apostolic fruits is an indicator of a lack of interior life, of a lack of friendship with God. The lukewarm

[11]J. Escrivá, *Friends of God*, 258.

person is virtually immobilized in his spiritual growth. He is like a train that had covered countless miles bearing plenty of cargo which all of sudden has come to a standstill on some forlorn siding. Its structure and cargo steadily deteriorate. Time passes and the elements take their toll. The train becomes more and more unfit for service. The same holds true for the interior life: *"He who does not advance, moves backward."*[12]

The person who succumbs to lukewarmness no longer profits from the abundant graces of the Holy Spirit. He becomes like the fig tree that disappointed Jesus: *"And seeing a fig tree by the wayside he went to it, and found nothing on it but leaves only. And he said to it, 'May no fruit ever come from you again!' And the fig tree withered at once."*[13] *"How deplorable. Does the same thing happen to us? Is the sad fact that we are lacking in faith, in dynamism in our humility? Have we no sacrifices, no good works to show? Is our Christianity just a facade, with nothing real behind it? (...) This Gospel passage makes us feel sorry, yet at the same time encourages us to strengthen our faith, to live by faith, so that we may always be ready to yield fruit to Our Lord...*

"What he wants are souls, he wants love. He wants all men to come to him, to enjoy his Kingdom forever. We have to work a lot on this earth and we must do our work well, since it is our daily tasks that we have to sanctify. But let us never forget to do everything for His sake. If we were to do it for ourselves, out of pride, we would produce nothing but leaves, and no matter how luxuriant they were, neither God nor our fellow men would find any good in them."[14]

Just as a falling rock accelerates as it gets closer to the ground, our love for God should increase as we draw closer

---

[12]St. Gregory the Great, *Pastoral Care*, 3, 34.
[13]Matt 21:19.
[14]J. Escrivá, *Friends of God*, 202.

to life's end. God wants us to make of our life a progressive communion with him.

Lukewarmness makes easy things difficult

The lukewarm person finds everything to be difficult. Yet for those who love, *"nothing is hard, nothing is difficult."*[15]

One day I saw four men carrying a large board. They were coming my way and soon I could tell that it was just a blackboard. Now a blackboard is not that heavy. It could have been carried by two people. But the four of them were carrying it and they were being worn out in the process!

As the workers drew closer, I could hear their moaning and complaining. *"This is so heavy!"* *"I'm carrying more of the weight than you are!"* *"You're just getting in the way!"* Thus they proceeded on their course, leaving behind a trail of ill humor. This job of hauling away the blackboard had evolved into a truly unpleasant ordeal.

I asked myself how something which weighed so little could end up being such a burden. Then I was reminded of how we Christians sometimes behave towards our obligations. We carry them out without love, without enthusiasm.

The lukewarm person does very little and yet complains a lot. He feels exhausted by the little that he does for God. And he almost always performs that little effort with bad humor. On the other hand, a person in love never balks at any sacrifice. He is always cheerful when he serves. St. Augustine teaches that *"in no way can the tasks of those who love be considered heavy."*[16] Truly, a visit to the Blessed Sacrament, a period of mental prayer, these can be pleasing

---

[15] St. Jerome, *Epistle*, 22, 40.
[16] St. Augustine, *De bono vitae*, 21, 26.

to the soul because it is therein meeting the Lord. They can also be a burden to someone who is merely fulfilling the letter of the law.

Love is the great motivator in the lives of the saints. Love gives us wings to fly over any obstacle in the interior life or apostolate. Love fortifies us in the face of trial. Lukewarmness leads us to become stuck on the smallest difficulties (that letter we have to write, that phone call, that visit, that conversation, that experience of poverty...). Lukewarmness makes a mountain out of a mole-hill. *"For I am sure that neither death, nor life, nor angels, nor principalities, nor things present, nor things to come, nor powers, nor height, nor depth, nor anything else in all creation, will be able to separate us from the love of God in Christ Jesus Our Lord."*[17]

Love for God transforms the soul and gives it new horizons. It makes the soul capable of new initiatives as it reveals unsuspected talents.

Next to Christ

Let us make a close reading of a familiar scene from the final chapter of St. John's Gospel.[18] After the death and Resurrection of Christ, the disciples had returned to Galilee just as the Lord had instructed them. The title "Lord" shows the deep reverence that they had for the Master. This title is repeated eight times in this section.

They were all back in their homeland (Judas was the only apostle not from Galilee). Some of the disciples were staying with Peter, namely, Thomas, Nathaniel, Andrew and John, plus two others who remain anonymous. The total, then, was seven.

[17]Rom 8:38-39.
[18]John 21:1 ff.

They were waiting for the Master's arrival. Meanwhile, they were working at their former trade: practically the entire group had been fishermen. This explains the suggestion made by Peter. *"Simon Peter said to them, 'I am going fishing.' They said to him, 'We will go with you.' They went out and got into the boat; but that night they caught nothing."*

It was dawn when they saw someone standing on the shore. They could not make out who it was. Maybe it was a townsperson waiting to buy some of their catch. *"The disciples did not know that it was Jesus."*

Jesus had come looking for Peter, as becomes evident as the story proceeds. He calls out to the disciples, *"Children, have you any fish?"* They answered him summarily, "No." This curt reply leads us to believe that the disciples had become somewhat discouraged.

Jesus then instructed them, *"Cast the net on the right side of the boat, and you will find some."* Peter recognized these words right away. He remembered that fateful day when Jesus borrowed his boat and then granted him an enormous catch of fish. On that same day He had also told the apostle to cast the net to the right side of the boat, even though they had spent the whole night without any success. It was on that day that Jesus had called Peter to be a *fisher of men*. It was a day he would never forget.

As these thoughts were going through Peter's mind, he obeyed the Lord's command and cast the net overboard. Perhaps he already knew that Jesus was standing there on the shore. *"So they cast it, and now they were not able to haul it all because of the quantity of the fish."*

It is John who first gives words to this exciting news. *"That disciple whom Jesus loved said to Peter, 'It is the Lord!'"* Peter then jumped into the water. *"When Simon Peter heard that it was the Lord, he put on his clothes, for he was stripped for work, and sprang into the sea."* The Lord was indeed waiting for him on the shore.

Soon afterwards the rest of the disciples came to shore with the boat full of fish, one hundred and fifty three of them. *"Although there were so many, the net was not torn."*

Let us pause and reflect for a moment on these verses which St. John has written with such great precision.

Standing on the shore of Lake Gennesaret, Jesus dominates the entire scene. He was more than one hundred yards away from the disciples when they were fishing. The whole night passed without any success. The disciples had wasted their time. When the morning comes, when Jesus becomes present to them, when the disciples hear his words and act accordingly, it is then that the nets are filled.

Every day the same thing happens to us. In the absence of Christ, day is night. Our work is sterile. Our efforts alone are insufficient. We need the help of God if we are to bear fruit.

When we live next to Christ, then our days are enriched beyond measure. Pain and sickness become wonderful treasures. As we sanctify our work, we are filling up the knapsack that we are carrying unto eternal life. We have so many opportunities to serve the people who work around us through our prayer, our encouragement, little deeds of service...

The tragedy comes when we no longer see Jesus. This may happen due to lukewarmness or pride. This is when we do things behind Christ's back, as it were. We pretend that Jesus never had a place in our life.

We have to make out the figure of the Lord on the shore. He is only one hundred yards away! We too have to shout forth: "It is the Lord!" We have to see him there in the midst of our ordinary affairs.

But at times we act like the Pharisees. Even though He is so near, we do not recognize him. That is surely the greatest tragedy. Our primary objective has to be to keep Christ in view. We cannot let our vision be obscured by neglect and pride. *"If we struggle daily to become saints, each of us in his own situation in the world and through his own job or profession, in our ordinary lives, then I assure you that God will make us into instruments that can work miracles and, if necessary, miracles of the most extraordinary kind. We will give sight to the blind. Who could not relate thousands of cases of people, blind almost from the day they were born, recovering their sight and receiving all the splendor of Christ's light? And others who were deaf, or dumb, who could not hear or pronounce words fitting to God's children... Their senses have been purified and now they listen and speak as men, not animals. 'In nomine Iesu!'* (Acts 3:7). *In the name of Jesus his Apostles enable the cripple to move and walk, when previously he had been incapable of doing anything useful; and that other lazy character, who knew his duties but didn't fulfill them... In the Lord's name, surge et ambula* (Acts 3:6), *'rise up and walk.'*

"Another man was dead, rotting, smelling like a corpse: he hears God's voice, as in the miracle of the son of the widow at Naim: 'Young man, I say to you, rise up' (Luke 7:14). *We will work miracles like Christ did, like the first apostles did. Maybe you yourself, and I, have benefited from such wonders. Perhaps we were blind, or deaf, or paralyzed; perhaps we had the stench of death, and the word of Our Lord has lifted us up from our abject state. If we love Christ, if we follow him sincerely, if we stop seeking ourselves and seek him alone, then in his name we will be able to give to others, freely, what we have freely received."*[19] Next to Christ, we shall be apostles in the middle of the world.

[19]J. Escrivá, *Friends of God*, 262.

XII

THE BEST REMEDY

"The love of our Mother will be the breath
that kindles into a living flame the embers
of virtue that are hidden under the ashes of
your indifference."[1]

The first miracle performed by Jesus, the one that manifested his glory and caused his disciples to believe in him,
had nothing to do with physical infirmity or diabolical
possession. The miracle was intended to save a couple of
newlyweds from embarrassment at their wedding feast. Of
all things that could go wrong, they had run out of wine.

Even though his hour had not yet come, Jesus granted
his Mother's request. Mary obtained an extraordinary grace
from her Son, as she would do again and again in the
centuries to follow. How many times we have felt ourselves
blessed as a result of her most powerful intercession!

The miracle was recorded for us by St. John.[2] He had
only recently joined the Master. "*On the third day there was
a marriage at Cana in Galilee, and the mother of Jesus was there;
Jesus was also invited to the marriage, with his disciples.*"

[1]J. Escrivá, *The Way*, 492.
[2]Cf. John 2:1-11.

"On the third day..." According to St. John's chronology, this refers to the calling of Philip three days before.

"And the mother of Jesus was there." St. John gives this fact a lot of importance. Her presence and her behavior are as significant as the miracle itself. Mary had probably come to the wedding from Nazareth, which entailed a journey of a little over four miles. She may have known this couple or she might have been related to either family in the wedding party. The statement that *"the mother of Jesus was there"* may be thought to suggest that Mary had arrived in Cana before her Son and his disciples. It is notable that the Evangelist makes no reference to Joseph in this account, even though he had previously mentioned that Joseph was the legal father of Jesus. The logical supposition from this silence is that Joseph had already passed away.[3]

It appears that Mary was actively involved in everything that pertained to the preparation of the feast. It was customary in the weddings held by the people of Palestine—even among the most important people—that the task of preparation fell to the sisters, relatives and friends of the bride. The Virgin must have been heavily involved since it was she who detected the looming problem before it leaked out to any of the invited guests. Not even the steward was aware of the shortage.

Jesus and Mary are now joined together after several months of separation. Jesus says very little, but we can imagine that both Mother and Son were happy to be united once more.

Then, suddenly, the unexpected happens. The wine runs out. Mary told her Son about the problem in a gentle prayer of petition. *"When the wine failed, the mother of Jesus said to him, 'They have no wine.' "* We are reminded of that petition which was later made by Martha and Mary of

---

[3]Cf. John 1:4-5.

Bethany: *"Lord, he whom you love is ill."*[4] It is to ask without asking. It is a prayer that is full of trust, a prayer that penetrates right to the soul of Jesus. This type of prayer is all-powerful.

And Jesus answers her: *"O woman, what have you to do with me? My hour has not come."*

If we are to truly understand this dialogue, we must have a sense of the gestures of Jesus and the tone of his remarks. For this dialogue was at once solemn, intimate and discrete. Everything is taking place in an atmosphere of familial gentleness. If we understand this dialogue in this way, then the words of the Lord make better sense. Otherwise, it would appear that Jesus had bruskly turned aside his Mother's petition. Yet Mary, who is his Mother after all, goes ahead and acts as if Jesus had assented. She tells the servants: *"Do whatever he tells you."*

We can imagine that the servants had witnessed this entire exchange. They were fully attentive to Mary's command. (How many times do we become so distracted that the opportunity to witness a miracle passes us by!)

So Jesus allows himself to be prevailed upon by his Mother. He thereby establishes a lasting precedent. Mary here becomes *omnipotencia suplicante,* the most powerful intercessor. Christians of every age have found Mary to be the 'short-cut' to Jesus. Thousands upon thousands of gifts and graces attest to this supernatural reality.

And Jesus says to the servants: *"Fill the jars with water."* The servants performed their assignment perfectly. *"They filled them up to the brim."* The quantity of water was enormous. Taking into consideration that each water jar held twenty or thirty gallons of fluid, the total volume of water must have been in the neighborhood of one hundred and fifty gallons. All of this was changed into wine. The

[4]John 11:3.

point being that Jesus was extremely generous with his Mother. This was true in terms of both quantity and quality. For Jesus turned the water into *excellent wine*.

The servants did their part faithfully. They filled up the jars with water—just ordinary, flavorless water. They had no other means at their disposal. But their meager resources serve to emphasize the power of Mary's intercession. They obeyed the Lord in what referred to the human means and, as a consequence, they made the miracle possible.

It is interesting to reflect on the fact that St. John recorded only six miracles in the course of his gospel. St. John was especially devoted to Mary, ever since Jesus told him, *"Behold your mother."*[5] He must have felt inspired to leave us this vivid account of Mary's intercession. *"Many conversions, many decisions to give oneself to the service of God have been preceded by an encounter with Mary. Our Lady has encouraged us to look for God, to desire to change, to lead a new life."*[6] It is impossible for lukewarmness to take root in a soul that is in love with the Virgin. For the Virgin prepares the heart to understand and befriend God. She inspires Christians to do apostolate, to be sincere in confession, to begin again. She will always obtain the grace we need to follow the Lord.

There is no better cure for lukewarmness, either to avoid it or to get out of it, than for a person to have a profound devotion to Mary.

Dealing with Mary

Some months later, when Jesus had already become somewhat famous for his teaching and miracles, a simple peasant woman started something that will not finish until the end of time. She sang the praises of Mary.

[5]John 19:27.
[6]J. Escrivá, *Christ is Passing By*, 149.

Jesus was speaking to the crowd. The people were all around him, soaking up his every word. All at once, this woman could not contain herself any more. She said to Jesus, *"Blessed is the womb that bore you, and the breasts that you sucked!"*[7]

Jesus then remembered his Mother and all that she had done to raise him. The praise of the woman must have greatly moved him.

The *Magnificat* had come to fruition. *"...henceforth all generations will call me blessed."* A peasant woman had thereupon begun something that will never stop until the end of the world. The Virgin's prophecy has been fulfilled throughout the centuries by poets, intellectuals, artisans, kings and warriors, men and women of mature age and children who have barely spoken their first words. Thousands of voices have sung praises to the Mother of Christ in the most diverse tongues.

Jesus takes advantage of this peasant woman's exclamation to give even greater praise to his Mother. *"But he said, 'Blessed rather are those who hear the word of God and keep it!'"*

No one ever listened to the word of God more attentively than Mary did. She kept it deep in her heart and faithfully put it into practice. Jesus praises the exemplary behavior of Mary and her love for the Will of God. The Church has always understood Christ's words in this light. This is why she has chosen these verses to precede the Gospel reading on certain feasts of Our Lady. *"It was a compliment to his Mother on her fiat (Luke 1:38), her 'be it done.' She lived it sincerely, unstintingly, fulfilling its every consequence, but never amid fanfare, rather in the hidden and silent sacrifice of each day."*[8]

[7]Luke 11:27-28.
[8]J. Escrivá, *Christ is Passing By*, 172.

Let us be grateful for the spontaneity of this woman.
And let us be grateful to St. Luke for being the one Evangelist who saved this incident for us.

We should be grateful because they both have taught
us an excellent way to praise and honor the Son of God: by
honoring his Mother. Jesus is delighted to hear praises for
his Mother.

It is easy to reach Christ through Mary. The Christian
people have always practiced this devotion, undoubtedly
because of the inspiration of the Holy Spirit. *"In a very
natural way we start wanting to speak to the Mother of God, who
is also our mother. We want to treat her as someone who is alive.
For death has not triumphed over her; she is body and soul in
the presence of God the Father, her Son, and the Holy Spirit...*

*"Our relationship with our own mother may show us how
to deal with Mary the Lady of the Sweet Name. We have to love
God with the same heart with which we love our parents, our
brothers and sisters, the other members of our family, our friends.
And we must love Mary with that same heart, too.*

*"How does a normal son or daughter treat his mother? In
different ways, of course, but always affectionately and confi-
dently, never coldly. In an intimate way, through small, common-
place customs. And a mother feels hurt if we omit them: a kiss
or an embrace when leaving or coming home, a little extra attention, a few warm words.*

*"In our relationship with our mother in Heaven, we should
act in very much the same way. Many Christians have the custom
of wearing the scapular; or they have acquired the habit of
greeting those pictures—a glance is enough—which are found
in every Christian home and in many public places; or they
recall the central events in Christ's life by saying the rosary,
never getting tired of repeating its words, just like people in love;
or they mark out a day of the week for her... doing some special
little thing for her and thinking particularly about her mother-
hood.*

*"There are many other Marian devotions which I needn't
mention here. A Christian doesn't need to live them all. (Growing
in supernatural life is not a matter of piling one devotion on top
of another.) I would say, however, that anyone who doesn't live
some of them, who doesn't express his love for Mary in some way,
does not possess the fullness of the faith.*

*"Those who think that devotions to Our Lady are a thing of
the past seem to have lost sight of the deep christian meaning they
contain. They seem to have forgotten the source from which they
spring: faith in God the Father's saving will; love for God the Son
who really became man and was born of a woman; trust in God
the Holy Spirit who sanctifies us with his grace. It is God who
has given us Mary, and we have no right to reject her. We should
go to her with a son's love and joy."*[9]

Whenever we feel weak, whenever we find ourselves
stalled or worn out or sluggish, let us go to Mary for help.
*"Let us then with confidence draw near to the throne of grace,
that we may receive mercy and find grace to help in time of
need."*[10] Let us love and venerate Our Lady because that is
the desire of the Lord. He has willed that we receive
everything through Mary.[11]

The joy of the Virgin

Christian joy is based on two things. First, that we are
fully convinced of God's love for us: *"So we know and believe
the love God has for us."*[12] And second, that we struggle daily
to grow in friendship with him. Fidelity means that we are
always ready to respond to new demands of love. A person

[9] J. Escrivá, *Christ is Passing By*, 142.
[10] Heb 4:16.
[11] Cf. St. Bernard, *De acquacd. serm.*, 6.
[12] 1 John 4:16.

cannot make his self-surrender conditional. Our vocation as Christian faithful begins at Baptism and it has to grow and mature in tandem with our personal development. We cannot put arbitrary limits on our dealings with God.

The Virgin is a model for us of joyful fidelity and love for God. At the Annunciation, the Angel Gabriel invited Mary to rejoice: *"Hail, full of grace, the Lord is with you!"*[13] The Virgin was filled with joy because of the proximity of the Lord. Elizabeth also proclaimed the Virgin's good fortune: *"Blessed is she who believed..."* Mary was able to rejoice because she said *"yes"* to God. *"My soul magnifies the Lord, and my spirit rejoices in God my Savior."*[14] These words reflect the wondrous grandeur of her immaculate soul which was so close to the Creator.

Mary's fidelity and, for that matter, her felicity are based on her detachment, her humility, her life of prayer, her docility and her abandonment to the Will of God. Her fidelity was put to the test in the most sorrowful moments of human history, there on Calvary.

The joy of the Redemption and the sorrow of the Cross are interwoven into the lives of Jesus and Mary. God wants to teach us that in this world real happiness is never far from contradiction and pain. This certainly was the lesson of Bethlehem where the joy of the Messiah's birth was tinged by privation and fear. The connection was also evident at the Presentation, in the flight to Egypt, in the finding of the Child Jesus in the Temple... Above all, this is the mystery of the Passion and Death of Mary's Son on the Cross. When at last his *hour* arrives, she contemplated his violated Body on the gibbet without complaint. Mary accepted her grief with serenity. She had a redemptive spirit that was intimately united to her Son.

[13]Cf. Luke 1:28.
[14]Luke 1:46-47.

Mary's fidelity was always growing throughout all the circumstances and events of her life. We see her with serene, trusting and silent joy as she fulfilled the Will of God in everything.

When we look at Mary, we should understand three critical truths. First, that our happiness lies in always saying *"yes"* to God. Second, that one has to be faithful to the Lord in all the circumstances of life. And third, that fidelity consists in complete detachment from our own plans and a complete attachment to the Will of God. Then we will make good headway on our journey to God.